Waheenee
An Indian Girl's Story

Waheenee, Gilbert Livingstone Wilson

Alpha Editions

This edition published in 2024

ISBN 9789362999474

Design and Setting By

Alpha Editions

www.alphaedis.com

Email - info@alphaedis.com

As per information held with us this book is in Public Domain.
This book is a reproduction of an important historical work.
Alpha Editions uses the best technology to reproduce historical work
in the same manner it was first published to preserve its original nature.
Any marks or number seen are left intentionally to preserve.

Contents

FOREWORD	- 1 -
FIRST CHAPTER	- 3 -
A LITTLE INDIAN GIRL	- 4 -
SECOND CHAPTER	- 13 -
WINTER CAMP	- 14 -
THIRD CHAPTER	- 21 -
THE BUFFALO-SKIN CAP	- 22 -
FOURTH CHAPTER	- 35 -
STORY TELLING	- 36 -
FIFTH CHAPTER	- 45 -
LIFE IN AN EARTH LODGE	- 46 -
SIXTH CHAPTER	- 56 -
CHILDHOOD GAMES AND BELIEFS	- 57 -
SEVENTH CHAPTER	- 68 -
KINSHIP, CLAN COUSINS	- 69 -
Story of Snake Head-Ornament	- 70 -
EIGHTH CHAPTER	- 76 -
INDIAN DOGS	- 77 -
NINTH CHAPTER	- 85 -
TRAINING A DOG	- 86 -
TENTH CHAPTER	- 93 -
LEARNING TO WORK	- 94 -
ELEVENTH CHAPTER	- 104 -
PICKING JUNE BERRIES	- 105 -
TWELFTH CHAPTER	- 115 -
THE CORN HUSKING	- 116 -
THIRTEENTH CHAPTER	- 124 -

MARRIAGE	- 125 -
FOURTEENTH CHAPTER	- 132 -
A BUFFALO HUNT	- 133 -
FIFTEENTH CHAPTER	- 144 -
THE HUNTING CAMP	- 145 -
SIXTEENTH CHAPTER	- 157 -
HOMEWARD BOUND	- 158 -
SEVENTEENTH CHAPTER	- 166 -
AN INDIAN PAPOOSE	- 167 -
EIGHTEENTH CHAPTER	- 174 -
THE VOYAGE HOME	- 175 -
AFTER FIFTY YEARS	- 184 -
GLOSSARY OF INDIAN WORDS	- 185 -
EXPLANATORY NOTES	- 187 -
SUPPLEMENT	- 194 -
HOW TO MAKE AN INDIAN CAMP	- 195 -
The Lodge	- 195 -
Booth	- 198 -
Fireplace	- 200 -
Broiling Meat	- 202 -
Drying Meat	- 202 -
Cooking Dried Meat	- 203 -
Parching Corn	- 203 -
HINTS TO YOUNG CAMPERS	- 206 -
INDIAN COOKING	- 207 -
EDITOR'S NOTE	- 209 -

FOREWORD

The Hidatsas, called Minitaris by the Mandans, are a Siouan tribe and speak a language closely akin to that of the Crows. Wars with the Dakota Sioux forced them to ally themselves with the Mandans, whose culture they adopted. Lewis and Clark found the two tribes living in five villages at the mouth of the Knife river, in 1804.

In 1832 the artist Catlin visited the Five Villages, as they were called. A year later Maximilian of Wiet visited them with the artist Bodmer. Several score canvasses, the work of the two artists, are preserved to us.

Smallpox nearly exterminated the two tribes in 1837-8. The survivors, a mere remnant, removed to Fort Berthold reservation where they still dwell.

In 1908, with my brother, an artist, I was sent by Dr. Clark Wissler, Curator of Anthropology, American Museum of Natural History, to begin cultural studies among the Hidatsas. This work, continued through successive summers for ten years, is but now drawing to a close.

During these years my faithful interpreter and helper has been Edward Goodbird, grandson of Small Ankle, a chief of the Hidatsas in the trying years following the terrible smallpox winter; and my principal informants have been Goodbird's mother, *Waheenee-wea*, or Buffalo-Bird Woman, and her brother, Wolf Chief.

The stories in this book were told me by Buffalo-Bird Woman. A few told in mere outline, have been completed from information given by Wolf Chief and others.

Illustrations are by my brother, from studies made by him on the reservation. They have been carefully compared with the Catlin and Bodmer sketches. Not a few are redrawn from cruder sketches by Goodbird, himself an artist of no mean ability.

Acknowledgment is made of the courtesy of Curator Wissler, whose permission makes possible the publishing of this book.

Indians have the gentle custom of adopting very dear friends by relationship terms. By such adoption Buffalo-Bird Woman is my mother. It is with real pleasure that I offer to young readers these stories from the life of my Indian mother.

G. L. W.

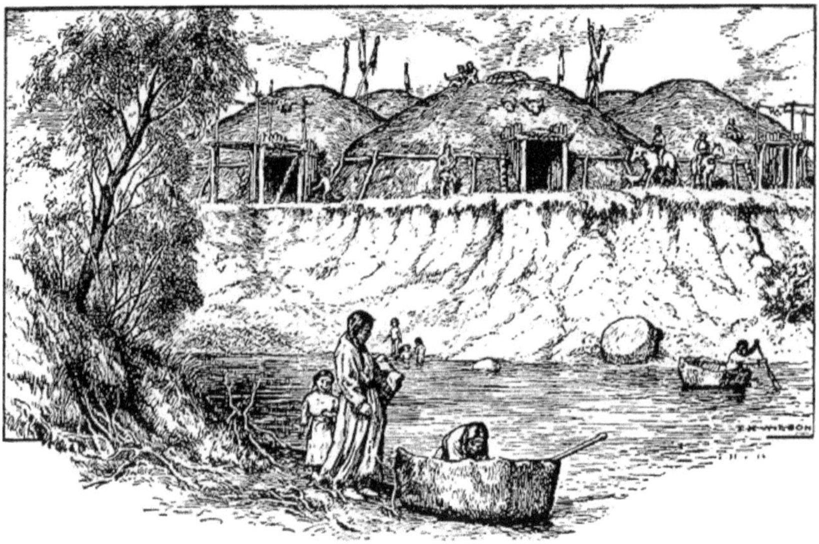

FIRST CHAPTER

A LITTLE INDIAN GIRL

I was born in an earth lodge by the mouth of the Knife river, in what is now North Dakota, three years after the smallpox winter.

The Mandans and my tribe, the Hidatsas, had come years before from the Heart river; and they had built the Five Villages, as we called them, on the banks of the Knife, near the place where it enters the Missouri.

Here were bottom lands for our cornfields and cottonwood trees for the beams and posts of our lodges. The dead wood that floated down either river would help keep us in firewood, the old women thought. Getting fuel in a prairie country was not always easy work.

When I was ten days old my mother made a feast and asked an old man named Nothing-but-Water to give me a name. He called me Good Way. "For I pray the gods," he said, "that our little girl may go through life by a *good way*; that she may grow up a good woman, not quarreling nor stealing; and that she may have good luck all her days."

I was a rather sickly child and my father wished after a time to give me a new name. We Indians thought that sickness was from the gods. A child's name was given him as a kind of prayer. A new name, our medicine men thought, often moved the gods to help a sick or weakly child.

So my father gave me another name, *Waheenee-wea*,[1] or Buffalo-Bird Woman. In our Hidatsa language, *waheenee*, means cowbird, or buffalo-bird, as this little brown bird is known in the buffalo country; *wea*, meaning girl or woman, is often added to a girl's name that none mistake it for the name of a boy. I do not know why my father chose this name. His gods, I know, were birds; and these, we thought, had much holy power. Perhaps the buffalo-birds had spoken to him in a dream.

[1] Wä hēē´ nēē wē´ a

I am still called by the name my father gave me; and, as I have lived to be a very old woman, I think it has brought me good luck from the gods.

My mother's name was *Weahtee*.[2] She was one of four sisters, wives of my father; her sisters' names were Red Blossom, Stalk-of-Corn, and Strikes-

Many Woman. I was taught to call all these my mothers. Such was our Indian custom. I do not think my mother's sisters could have been kinder to me if I had been an own daughter.

[2] Wē´ äh tēē

I remember nothing of our life at the Five Villages; but my great-grandmother, White Corn, told me something of it. I used to creep into her bed when the nights were cold and beg for stories.

"The Mandans lived in two of the villages, the Hidatsas in three," she said. "Around each village, excepting on the side that fronted the river, ran a fence of posts, with spaces between for shooting arrows. In front of the row of posts was a deep ditch.

"We had corn aplenty and buffalo meat to eat in the Five Villages, and there were old people and little children in every lodge. Then smallpox came. More than half of my tribe died in the smallpox winter. Of the Mandans only a few families were left alive. All the old people and little children died."

I was sad when I heard this story. "Did any of your family die, grandmother?" I asked.

"Yes, my husband, Yellow Elk, died. So many were the dead that there was no time to put up burial scaffolds; so his clan fathers bore Yellow Elk to the burying ground and laid him on the grass with logs over him to keep off the wolves.

"That night the villagers heard a voice calling to them from the burying ground. '*A-ha-hey!*[3] I have waked up. Come for me.'

[3] Ä hä hey´

"'It is a ghost,' the villagers cried; and they feared to go.

"Some brave young men, listening, thought they knew Yellow Elk's voice. They went to the burying ground and called, 'Are you alive, Yellow Elk?'

"'Yes,' he answered, 'I have waked up!'

"The young men rolled the logs from his body and bore Yellow Elk to the village; he was too weak to walk."

This story of Yellow Elk I thought wonderful; but it scared me to know that my great-grandfather had been to the ghost land and had come back again.

Enemies gave our tribes much trouble after the smallpox year, my grandmother said. Bands of Sioux waylaid hunting parties or came prowling around our villages to steal horses. Our chiefs, Mandan and Hidatsa, held a council and decided to remove farther up the Missouri. "We will build a new village," they agreed, "and dwell together as one tribe."

The site chosen for the new village was a place called Like-a-Fishhook Point, a bit of high bench land that jutted into a bend of the Missouri. We set out for our new home in the spring, when I was four years old. I remember nothing of our march thither. My mothers have told me that not many horses were then owned by the Hidatsas, and that robes, pots, axes, bags of corn and other stuff were packed on the backs of women or on travois dragged by dogs.

The march was led by the older chiefs and medicine men. My grandfather was one of them. His name was Missouri River. On the pommel of his saddle hung his medicines, or sacred objects, two human skulls wrapped in a skin. They were believed to be the skulls of thunder birds, who, before they died, had changed themselves into Indians. After the chiefs, in a long line, came warriors, women, and children. Young men who owned ponies were sent ahead to hunt meat for the evening camp. Others rode up and down the line to speed the stragglers and to see that no child strayed off to fall into the hands of our enemies, the Sioux.

The earth lodges that the Mandans and Hidatsas built, were dome-shaped houses of posts and beams, roofed over with willows-and-grass, and earth; but every family owned a tepee, or skin tent, for use when hunting or traveling. Our two tribes camped in these tents the first summer at Like-a-Fishhook Point, while they cleared ground for cornfields.

The labor of clearing was done chiefly by the women, although the older men helped. Young men were expected to be off fighting our enemies or hunting buffaloes. There was need for hunting. Our small, first year's fields could yield no large crops; and, to keep from going hungry in the winter months, we must lay in a good store of dried meat. We owned few guns in the tribe then; and hunting buffaloes with arrows was anything but sport. Only young men, strong and active, made good hunters.

My mothers were hard-working women, and began their labor of clearing a field almost as soon as camp was pitched. My grandmother, Turtle, chose the ground for the field. It was in a piece of bottom land that lay along the river, a little east of the camp. My mothers had brought seed corn from the Five Villages; and squash, bean and sunflower seed.

I am not sure that they were able to plant much corn the first season. I know they planted some beans and a few squashes. I am told that when the squash harvest came in, my grandmother picked out a long green-striped squash for me, for a doll baby. I carried this about on my back, snuggled under my buffalo-calf robe, as I had seen Indian mothers carry their babies. At evening I wrapped my dolly in a bit of skin and put her to bed.

Our camp on a summer's evening was a cheerful scene. At this hour, fires burned before most of the tepees; and, as the women had ended their day's labors, there was much visiting from tent to tent. Here a family sat eating their evening meal. Yonder, a circle of old men, cross-legged or squat-on-heels in the firelight, joked and told stories. From a big tent on one side of the camp came the *tum-tum tum-tum* of a drum. We had dancing almost every evening in those good days.

But for wee folks bedtime was rather early. In my father's family, it was soon after sunset. My mothers had laid dry grass around the tent wall, and on this had spread buffalo skins for beds. Small logs, laid along the edge of the beds, caught any sparks from the fireplace; for, when the nights grew chill, my mothers made their fire in the tepee. My father often sat and sang me to sleep by the firelight.

He had many songs. Some of them were for little boys: others were for little girls. Of the girls' songs, there was one I liked very much; it was something like this:

My sister asks me to go out and stretch the smoke-flap.

My armlets and earrings shine!

I go through the woods where the elm trees grow.

Why do the berries not ripen?

What berries do you like best?—the red? the blue?

This song I used to try to sing to my squash doll, but I found it hard to remember the words.

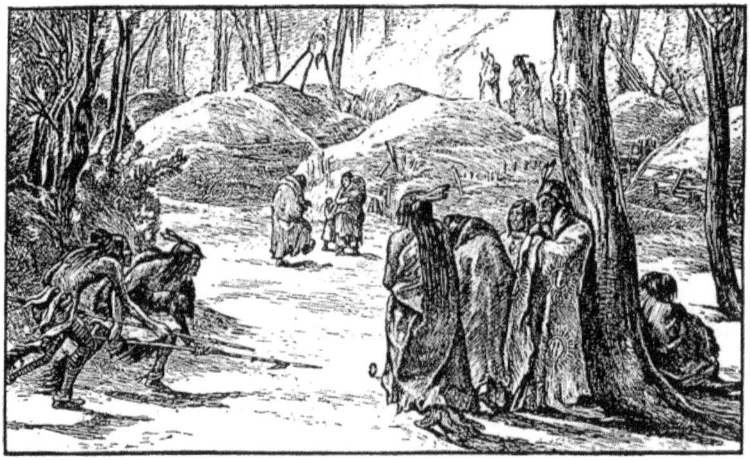

SECOND CHAPTER

WINTER CAMP

The medicine men of the two tribes had laid out the plan of our new village when they made camp in the spring. There was to be an open circle in the center, with the lodges of the chiefs and principal men opening upon it; and in the center of the circle was to stand the Mandans' sacred corral. This corral was very holy. Around it were held solemn dances, when young men fasted and cut their flesh to win favor of the gods.

The early planning of the village by our medicine men made it possible for a woman to choose a site and begin building her earth lodge. Few lodges, however, were built the first summer. My mothers did not even begin building theirs; but they got ready the timbers with which to frame it.

Going often into the woods with their dogs to gather firewood, they kept a sharp lookout for trees that would make good beams or posts; these they felled later, and let lie to cure. For rafters, they cut long poles; and from cottonwood trunks they split puncheons for the sloping walls. In olden days puncheons were split with wedges of buffalo horn. A core of hard ash wood was driven into the hollow horn to straighten it and make it solid.

Autumn came; my mothers harvested their rather scanty crops; and, with the moon of Yellow Leaves, we struck tents and went into winter camp. My tribe usually built their winter village down in the thick woods along the Missouri, out of reach of the cold prairie winds. It was of earth lodges, like those of our summer village, but smaller and more rudely put together. We made camp this winter not very far from Like-a-Fishhook Point.

My father's lodge, or, better, my mothers' lodge,—for an earth lodge belonged to the women who built it—was more carefully constructed than most winter lodges were. Earth was heaped thick on the roof to keep in the warmth; and against the sloping walls without were leaned thorny rosebushes, to keep the dogs from climbing up and digging holes in the roof. The fireplace was a round, shallow pit, with edges plastered smooth with mud. Around the walls stood the family beds, six of them, covered each with an old tent skin on a frame of poles.

A winter lodge was never very warm; and, if there were old people or children in the family, a second, or "twin lodge," was often built. This was a small lodge with roof peaked like a tepee, but covered with bark and earth. A covered passage led from it to the main lodge.

The twin lodge had two uses. In it the grandparents or other feeble or sickly members of the family could sit, snug and warm, on the coldest day; and the children of the household used it as a playhouse.

I can just remember playing in our twin lodge, and making little feasts with bits of boiled tongue or dried berries that my mothers gave me. I did not often get to go out of doors; for I was not a strong little girl, and, as the winter was a hard one, my mothers were at pains to see that I was kept warm. I had a tiny robe, made of a buffalo-calf skin, that I drew over my little buckskin dress; and short girls' leggings over my ankles. In the twin lodge, as in the larger earth lodge, the smoke hole let in plenty of fresh air.

My mothers had a scant store of corn and beans, and some strings of dried squashes; and they had put by two or three sacks of dried prairie turnips. A mess of these turnips was boiled now and then and was very good. Once, I remember, we had a pudding, dried prairie turnips pounded to a meal and boiled with dried June berries. Such a pudding was sweet, and we children were fond of it.

To eke out our store of corn and keep the pot boiling, my father hunted much of the time. To hunt deer he left the lodge before daybreak, on snowshoes, if the snow was deep. He had a flintlock gun, a smoothbore with a short barrel. The wooden stock was studded with brass nails. For shot he used slugs, bits of lead which he cut from a bar, and chewed to make round like bullets. Powder and shot were hard to get in those days.

Buffaloes were not much hunted in winter, when they were likely to be poor in flesh; but my father and his friends made one hunt before midwinter set in. Buffaloes were hunted with bow and arrows, from horseback. Only a fleet pony could overtake a buffalo, and there were not many such owned in the tribe. We thought a man rich who had a good buffalo horse.

My father stabled his horses at night in our lodge, in a little corral fenced off against the wall. "I do not want the Sioux to steal them," he used to say. In the morning, after breakfast, he drove them out upon the prairie, to pasture, but brought them in again before sunset. In very cold weather my mothers cut down young cottonwoods and let our horses browse on the tender branches.

Early in the spring our people returned to Like-a-Fishhook Point and took up again the labor of clearing and planting fields. Each family had its own field, laid out in the timbered bottom lands along the Missouri, if possible, in a rather open place where there were no large trees to fell.

Felling trees and grubbing out bushes were done with iron tools, axes and heavy hoes, gotten of the traders. I have heard that in old times my tribe used stone axes, but I never saw them myself. Our family field was larger than any owned by our neighbors; and my mothers were at pains to add to it, for they had many mouths to feed. My grandmother, Turtle, helped them, rising at the first sound of the birds to follow my mothers to the field.

Turtle was old-fashioned in her ways and did not take kindly to iron tools. "I am an Indian," she would say, "I use the ways my fathers used." Instead of grubbing out weeds and bushes, she pried them from the ground with a wooden digging stick. I think she was as skillful with this as were my mothers with their hoes of iron.

Digging sticks are even yet used by old Hidatsa women for digging wild turnips. The best kind is made of a stout ash sapling, slightly bent and trimmed at the root end to a three-cornered point. To harden the point, it is oiled with marrow fat, and a bunch of dry grass is tied around it and fired. The charring makes the point almost as hard as iron.

Turtle, I think, was the last woman in the tribe to use an old-fashioned, bone-bladed hoe. Two other old women owned such hoes, but no longer used them in the fields. Turtle's hoe was made of the shoulder bone of a buffalo set in a light-wood handle, the blade firmly bound in place with thongs. The handle was rather short, and so my grandmother stooped as she worked among her corn hills.

She used to keep the hoe under her bed. As I grew a bit older my playmates and I thought it a curious old tool, and sometimes we tried to take it out and look at it, when Turtle would cry, "*Nah, nah!*[4] Go away! Let that hoe alone; you will break it!"

[4] Näh

We children were a little afraid of Turtle.

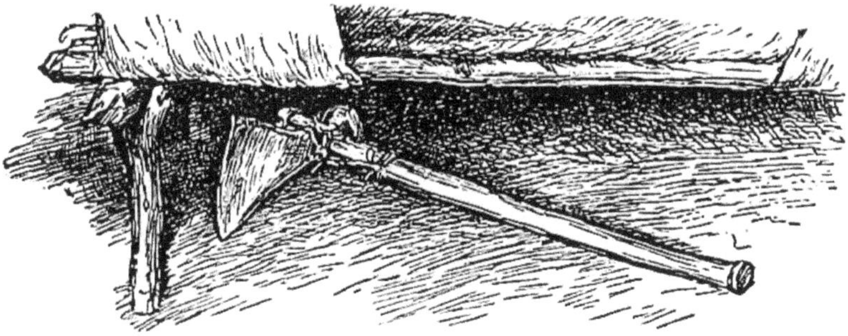

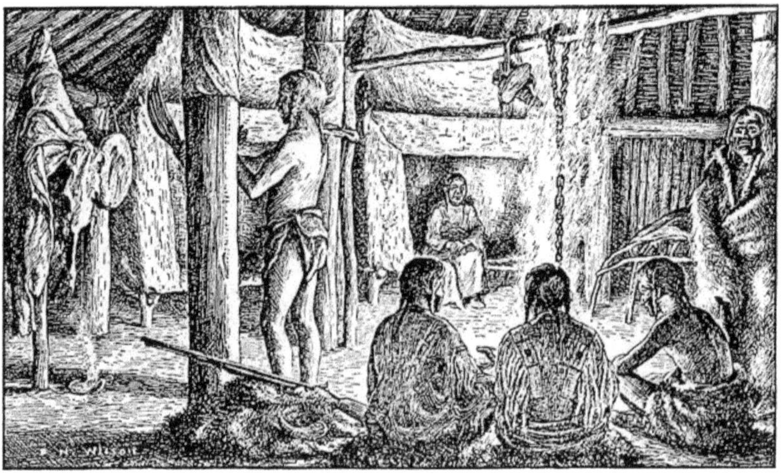

THIRD CHAPTER

THE BUFFALO-SKIN CAP

The winter I was six years old my mother, *Weahtee*, died.

The Black Mouths, a men's society, had brought gifts to One Buffalo and asked him to be winter chief. "We know you own sacred objects, and have power with the gods," they said. "We want you to pray for us and choose the place for our camp."

One Buffalo chose a place in the woods at the mouth of Many-Frogs Brook, three miles from Like-a-Fishhook village. I remember our journey thither. There was a round, open place in the trees by Many-Frogs Brook, where young men fasted and made offerings to the gods. It was a holy place; and One Buffalo thought, if we pitched our winter camp near-by, the gods would remember us and give us a good winter.

But it was a hard winter from its start. Cold weather set in before we had our lodges well under cover; and, with the first snow, smallpox broke out in camp. Had it been in summer, my tribe could have broken up into small bands and scattered; and the smallpox would have died out. This they could not do in winter, and many died. My brother, my mother *Weahtee*, and her sister Stalk-of-Corn, died, of my father's family.

Although my old grandmother was good to me, I often wept for my mother. I was lonesome in our winter lodge, and we Indian children did not have many playthings. Old Turtle made me a dolly of deer skin stuffed with antelope hair. She sewed on two white bone beads for eyes. I bit off one of these bone beads, to see if it was good to eat, I suppose. For some days my dolly was one-eyed, until my grandmother sewed on a beautiful new eye, a blue glass bead she had gotten of a trader. I thought this much better, for now my dolly had one blue eye and one white one.

I liked to play with my father's big hunting cap. It was made of buffalo skin, from the part near the tail where the hair is short. He wore it with the fur side in. Two ears of buffalo skin, stuffed with antelope hair to make them stand upright, were sewed one on each side. They were long, to look like a jack rabbit's ears; but they looked more like the thumbs of two huge mittens. My father, I think, had had a dream from the jack-rabbit spirits, and wore the cap as a kind of prayer to them. Jack rabbits are hardy animals and fleet of foot. They live on the open prairies through the hardest winters; and a full grown rabbit can outrun a wolf. An Indian hunter had need to be nimble-footed and hardy, like a jack rabbit.

Small Ankle thought his cap a protection in other ways. It kept his head warm. Then, if he feared enemies were about, he could draw his cap down to hide his dark hair, creep up a hill and spy over the top. Being of dull color, like dead grass, the cap was not easily seen on the sky line. A Sioux, spying it, would likely think it a coyote, or wolf, with erect, pointed ears, peering over the hill, as these animals often did. There were many such caps worn by our hunters; but most of them had short pointed ears, like a coyote's.

My father sometimes hung his cap, wet with snow, on the drying poles over the fire to dry. I would watch it with longing eyes; and, when I thought it well warmed, I would hold up my small hands and say, "Father, let me play with the cap." I liked to sit in it, my small ankles turned to the right, like an Indian woman's; for I liked the feel of the warm fur against my bare knees. At other times I marched about the lodge, the big cap set loosely on my head, and my dolly thrust under my robe on my back. In doing this I always made my grandmother laugh. "Hey, hey," she would cry, "that is a warrior's cap. A little girl can not be a warrior."

The winter, if hard, was followed by an early spring. Snow was thawing and flocks of wild geese were flying north a month before their wonted time. The women of the Goose Society called the people for their spring dance, and prayed the gods for good weather for the corn planting. One Buffalo sent a crier through the lodges, warning us to make ready to break camp. On the day set, we all returned to Like-a-Fishhook village, glad to leave our stuffy little winter lodges for our roomy summer homes.

One morning, shortly after our return, my father came into the lodge with two brave men, Flying Eagle and Stuck-by-Fish. My grandfather, Big Cloud, joined them. Big Cloud lighted a pipe, offered smoke to the gods, and passed the pipe to the others. It was a long pipe with black stone bowl. The four men talked together. I heard my father speak of a war party and that he was sure his gods were strong.

Toward evening, Red Blossom boiled meat and set it before the men. When they had eaten, Small Ankle rose and went to his medicine bag, that hung in the rear of the lodge. He held out his hands and I saw his lips move; and I knew he was praying. He opened the medicine bag and took out a bundle which he unrolled. It was a black bear's skin, painted red. He bore the skin reverently out of the lodge, and came back empty-handed. Flying Eagle and Stuck-by-Fish rose and left the lodge.

My father sat by the fire awhile, silent. Then from a post of his bed he fetched his hunting cap. "I shall need this cap," he said to Red Blossom. "See if it must be sewed or mended in any place."

The next morning when I went out of the lodge, I saw that the black-bear skin was bound to one of the posts at the entrance. This was a sign that my father was going to lead out a war party. I was almost afraid to pass the bear skin, for I knew it was very holy.

For days after, young men came to our lodge to talk with my father and Big Cloud. My mothers—for so I called Red Blossom and Strikes-Many Woman—had the pot boiling all the time, to give food to the young warriors.

One night I was in bed and asleep, when I woke with a start, hearing low voices. Peeping out, I saw many young men sitting around the fireplace. The fire had died down, but the night was clear and a little light came through the smoke hole. Many of the young men had bows and well-filled quivers on their backs. A few had guns.

Some one struck flint and steel, and I saw by the glow of the burning tobacco that a pipe was being passed. The men were talking low, almost in whispers. Then I heard Big Cloud's voice, low and solemn, praying: "Oh gods, keep watch over these our young men. Let none of them be harmed. Help them strike many enemies and steal many horses."

The company now arose and filed out of the lodge. As the skin door fell shut after them, I heard the whinny of Small Ankle's war pony without. Next morning, I learned that Small Ankle and Big Cloud had led out a war party, all mounted, to strike the northern Sioux.

The ice on the Missouri river broke, and ran out with much crashing and roaring. Some dead buffaloes, frozen in the ice, came floating down the current. Our brave young men, leaping upon the ice cakes, poled the carcasses to shore. We were glad to get such carcasses. Buffaloes killed in the spring were lean and poor in flesh; but these, frozen in the ice, were fat and tender.

A good many frozen carcasses were thus taken at the spring break-up. In the fall the rivers froze over, often with rather thin ice. A herd would come down to the river's edge and stand lowing and grumbling, until some bold bull walked out upon the ice. The whole herd followed, often breaking through with their weight.

The weather stayed warm. Bushes in the woods had begun to leaf, and old Turtle even raked part of our field and planted sunflower seed around the border. "We never saw such an early spring," said some of the old men.

Then, one night, a cold wind arose with rain turning to snow. I woke up, crying out that I was chilled. My grandmother, who slept with me, pulled over us an extra robe she had laid up on the top of the bed frame.

The next morning a terrible blizzard broke over our village. The wind howled overhead, driving the falling snow in blinding clouds. Red Blossom drew her robe over her head and went to the entrance to run over to our next neighbor's; but she came back. "I am afraid to go out," she said. "The air is so full of snow that I can not see my hand when I hold it before my face. I fear I might lose my way, and wander out on the prairie and die." There were stories in the tribe of villagers who had perished thus.

Old Turtle and Strikes-Many Woman made ready our noon meal—no easy thing to do; for the cold wind, driving down the smoke hole, blew ashes into our faces and into our food. An old bull-boat frame was turned over the smoke hole. Against it, on the windward side, my mothers had laid a buffalo skin the night before, weighting it down with a stone. This was to keep the wind from blowing smoke down the smoke hole; but the wind had shifted in the night, blowing the buffalo skin off the boat frame. The weight of the stone had sunk one end of the skin into the earth roof, where it had frozen fast; and we could hear the loose end flapping and beating in the wind. Little snow came down the smoke hole. The wind was so strong that it carried the snow off the roof.

Turtle and Strikes-Many Woman had gone with dogs for firewood only the day before; so there was plenty of fuel in the lodge. We could not go to get water at the river; but Red Blossom crept into the entrance way and filled a skin basket with snow. This she melted in a clay pot, for water. It was in this water that we boiled our meat for the midday meal. In spite of the calf skin that my grandmother belted about me, I shivered with the cold until my teeth chattered. Turtle poured some of the meat broth, steaming hot, into a wooden bowl, and fetched me a buffalo-horn spoon. With this spoon I scooped up the broth, glad to swallow something hot into my cold little stomach.

After our meal, my two mothers and Turtle sat on my father's couch, looking grave. "I hope Small Ankle and Big Cloud have reached shelter in the Missouri-river timber," I heard Red Blossom say. "If they are on the prairie in this storm, they will die."

"Big Cloud's prayers are strong," answered Turtle, "and Small Ankle is a good plainsman. I am sure they and their party will find shelter."

"I knew a Mandan who was caught in a blizzard," said Red Blossom. "He walked with the wind until he fell into a coulee, that was full of snow. He burrowed under the drifts and lay on his back, with his knees doubled against his chin and his robe tight about him. He lay there three days, until the storm blew over. He had a little parched corn for food; and, for drink, he ate snow. He came home safely; but his mouth was sore from the snow he had eaten."

Darkness came early, with the wind still screaming overhead. Turtle tried to parch some corn in a clay pot, but blasts from the smoke hole blew ashes into her eyes. She took out a handful of the half-parched corn, when it had cooled, and poured it into my two hands. This was my supper; but she also gave me a lump of dried chokecherries to eat. They were sweet and I was fond of them.

I awoke the next morning to see my mothers cooking our breakfast, parched-corn meal stirred into a thick mush with beans and marrow fat. I sprang out of bed and glanced up at the smoke hole. The sky, I saw, was clear and the sun was shining.

The second day after, about midafternoon, Small Ankle came home. I heard the tinkle of the hollow hoofs that hung on the skin door, and in a moment my father came around the fire screen leading his war pony, a bay with a white nose. He put his pony in the corral, replaced the bar, and came over to his couch by the fire. My mothers said nothing. Red Blossom put water and dried meat in a pot and set it on the fire, and Turtle fetched an armful of green cottonwood bark to feed the pony.

My father took off his big cap and hung it on the drying pole, and wrung out his moccasins and hung them beside the cap. They were winter moccasins, and in each was a kind of stocking, of buffalo skin turned fur in, and cut and sewed to fit snugly over the foot. These stockings Small Ankle drew out and laid by the fire, to dry. He put on dry moccasins, threw off his robe, and took upon his knees the bowl of broth and meat that Red Blossom silently handed him.

In the evening, some of his cronies came in to smoke and talk. Small Ankle told them of his war party.

"We had a hard time," he said. "Perhaps the gods, for some cause, were angry with us. We had gone five days; evening came and it began to rain. We were on the prairie, and our young men sat all night with their saddles and saddle skins over their heads to keep off the rain.

"In the morning, the rain turned to snow. A heavy wind blew the snow in our faces, nearly blinding us.

"'We must make our way to the Missouri timber and find shelter,' Big Cloud said.

"Flying Eagle feared we could not find our way. 'The air is so full of snow that we can not see the hills,' he said.

"'The wind will guide us,' said Stuck-by-Fish. 'We know the Missouri river is in the south. The wind is from the west. If we travel with the wind on our right, we shall be headed south. We should reach the river before night.'

"I thought this a good plan, and I cried, 'My young men, saddle your horses.' We had flat saddles, such as hunters use. We had a few bundles of dried meat left. These we bound firmly to our saddles, for we knew we could kill no game while the storm lasted.

"Many of my young men had head cloths which they bound over their hair and under their chins; but the wind was so strong that it blew the wet snow through the cloths, freezing them to the men's faces. I had on my fur cap, which kept my face warm. Also, I think the jack-rabbit spirits helped me.

"We pushed on; but the snow got deeper and deeper until we could hardly force our ponies through it. We grew so chilled that Big Cloud ordered us to dismount and go afoot. 'You go first,' he said to Flying Eagle. 'You are a tall man and have long legs. You break the way through the snow. We will follow single-file.'

"Flying Eagle did so, leading his pony. With Flying Eagle had come his brother, Short Buffalo, a lad of fourteen or fifteen years. He was not yet grown, and his legs were so short that he could not make his way through the deep snow. We let him ride.

"But in a little while Short Buffalo cried out, 'My brother, I freeze; I die!'

"Flying Eagle called back, 'Do not give up, little brother. Be strong!' And he came back and bound Short Buffalo's robe snugly about his neck, and took the reins of his pony, so that Short Buffalo could draw his hands under his robe to warm them. Short Buffalo's robe had frozen stiff in the cold wind.

"We reached the Missouri before nightfall and went down into the thick timber. It was good to be out of the freezing wind, sheltered by the trees.

"Flying Eagle led us to a point of land over which had swept a fire, killing the trees. Many dead cottonwoods stood there, with shaggy bark. We peeled off the thick outer bark, shredding the dry inner bark for tinder. I had flint and steel. We rolled over a fallen trunk and started a fire on the dry ground beneath. We broke off dead branches for fuel.

"Flying Eagle helped me get wood and start the fire. He is a strong man and bore the cold better than the others. Many of the men were too benumbed to help any. My mittens and my cap had kept me warm.

"The men's leggings, wetted by rain and snow, were frozen stiff. We soon had a hot fire. When their leggings had thawed soft, the men took off these and their moccasins, and wrung them out; and when they had half dried them by the fire, put them on again. They also put shredded cottonwood bark in their moccasins, packing it about their feet and ankles to keep them warm and dry.

"We toasted dried meat over the fire, and ate; for we were hungry, and weak from the cold. We fed our ponies green cottonwood branches that we cut with our knives.

"The storm died down before morning; and early the next day we started down the river to our village. We were slow coming, for the snow thawed, growing soft and slushy under our ponies' feet. Our ponies, too, were weak from the cold."

Many of the young men of my father's party had their faces frozen on the right side. Short Buffalo had part of his right hand frozen, and his right foot. He was sick for a long time. Another war party that had been led out by Wooden House had also been caught in the storm and had fared even worse. They were afoot, and, not being able to reach the river timber, they lay down in a coulee and let the snow drift over them. Two were frozen to death.

The leaders of a war party were held to blame for any harm that came to their men. The villagers, however, did not blame my father much. Some of the older men said, "Small Ankle and Big Cloud were foolish. The wild geese had come north, but this fact alone was not proof that winter had gone. We know that bad storms often blow up at this season of the year."

Of course, being but six years old, I could hardly remember all these things. But my father talked of his war party many times afterwards, at his evening fire, as he smoked with his cronies; and so I came to know the story.

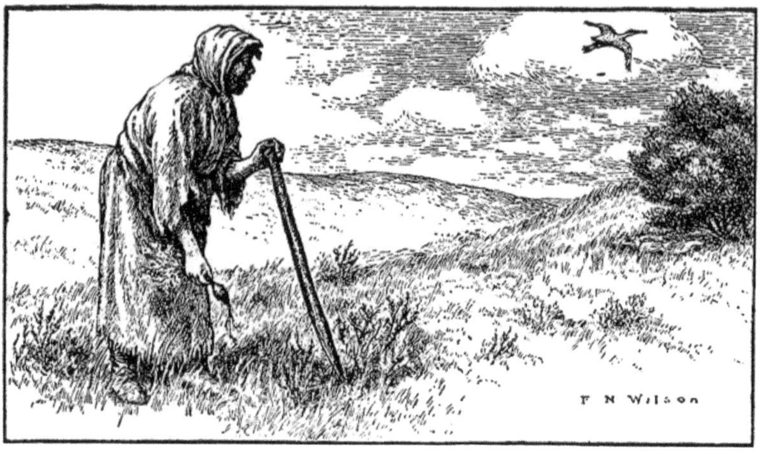
F N Wilson

FOURTH CHAPTER

STORY TELLING

My good old grandmother could be stern when I was naughty; nevertheless, I loved her dearly, and I know she was fond of me. After the death of my mother, it fell to Turtle to care for me much of the time. There were other children in the household, and, with so many mouths to feed, my two other mothers, as I called them, had plenty of work to do.

Indians are great story tellers; especially are they fond of telling tales around the lodge fire in the long evenings of autumn and winter. My father and his cronies used sometimes to sit up all night, drumming and singing and telling stories. Young men often came with gift of robe or knife, to ask him to tell them tales of our tribe.

I was too young yet to understand many of these tales. My father was hours telling some of them, and they had many strange words. But my grandmother used to tell me stories as she sat or worked by the lodge fire.

One evening in the corn planting moon, she was making ready her seed for the morrow's planting. She had a string of braided ears lying beside her. Of these ears she chose the best, broke off the tip and butt of each, and shelled the perfect grain of the mid-cob into a wooden bowl. Baby-like, I ran my fingers through the shiny grain, spilling a few kernels on the floor.

"Do not do that," cried my grandmother. "Corn is sacred; if you waste it, the gods will be angry."

I still drew my fingers through the smooth grain, and my grandmother continued: "Once a Ree woman went out to gather her corn. She tied her robe about her with a big fold in the front, like a pocket. Into this she dropped the ears that she plucked, and bore them off to the husking pile. All over the field she went, row by row, leaving not an ear.

"She was starting off with her last load when she heard a weak voice, like a babe's, calling, 'Please, please do not go. Do not leave me.'

"The woman stopped, astonished. She put down her load. 'Can there be a babe hidden in the corn?' she thought. She then carefully searched the field, hill by hill, but found nothing.

"She was taking up her load, when again she heard the voice: 'Oh, please do not go. Do not leave me!' Again she searched, but found nothing.

"She was lifting her load when the voice came the third time: 'Please, please, do not go! Please, do not leave me!'

"This time the woman searched every corn hill, lifting every leaf. And lo, in one corner of the field, hidden under a leaf, she found a tiny nubbin of yellow corn. It was the nubbin that had been calling to her. For so the gods would teach us not to be wasteful of their gifts."

Another evening I was trying to parch an ear of corn over the coals of our lodge fire. I had stuck the ear on the end of a squash spit, as I had seen my mothers do; but my baby fingers were not strong enough to fix the ear firmly, and it fell off into the coals and began to burn. My mouth puckered, and I was ready to cry.

My grandmother laughed. "You should put only half the ear on the spit," she said. "That is the way the Mandans did when they first gave us corn."

I dropped the spit and, forgetting the burning ear, asked eagerly, "How did the Mandans give us corn, grandmother? Tell me the story."

Turtle picked up the spit and raked the burning ear from the ashes. "I have told you that the gods gave us corn to eat, not to waste," she said. "Some of the kernels on this cob are well parched." And she shelled off a handful and put one of the hot kernels in her mouth.

"I will tell you the story," she continued. "I had it from my mother when I was a little girl like you.

"In the beginning, our Hidatsa people lived under the waters of Devils Lake. They had earth lodges and lived much as we live now. One day some hunters found the root of a grapevine growing down from the lake overhead. They climbed the vine and found themselves on this earth. Others climbed the vine until half the tribe had escaped; but, when a fat woman tried to climb it, the vine broke, leaving the rest of the tribe under the lake.

"Those who had safely climbed the vine, built villages of earth lodges. They lived by hunting; and some very old men say that they also planted small fields in ground beans and wild potatoes. As yet the Hidatsas knew nothing of corn or squashes.

"One day, a war party that had wandered west to the Missouri river saw on the other side a village of earth lodges like their own. It was a village of the Mandans. Neither they nor the Hidatsas would cross over, each party fearing the other might be enemies.

"It was in the fall of the year, and the Missouri was running low, so that an arrow could be shot from shore to shore. The Mandans parched some ears of ripe corn with the grain on the cob. These ears they broke in pieces, stuck the pieces on the points of arrows and shot them across the river. 'Eat!' they called. The word for 'eat' is the same in both the Hidatsa and the Mandan languages.

"The Hidatsas ate of the parched corn. They returned to their village and said, 'We have found a people on a great river, to the west. They have a strange kind of grain. We ate of it and found it good.'

"After this, a party of Hidatsas went to visit the Mandans. The Mandan chief took an ear of corn, broke it in two, and gave half to the Hidatsas for seed. This half ear the Hidatsas took home, and soon every family in the village was planting corn."

My father had been listening, as he sat smoking on the other side of the fire. "I know that story," he said. "The name of the Mandan chief was Good-Fur Robe."

My grandmother then put me to bed. I was so sleepy that I did not notice she had eaten up all the corn I had parched.

Winter came again, and spring. As soon as the soil could be worked, my mothers and old Turtle began cleaning up our field, and breaking new ground to add to it. Our first year's field had been small; but my mothers added to it each season, until the field was as large as our family needed.

I was too little to note very much of what was done. I remember that my father set up boundary marks—little piles of earth or stones, I think they were—to mark the corners of the field we claimed. My mothers and Turtle began at one end of the field and worked forward. My mothers had their heavy iron hoes; and Turtle, her old-fashioned digging stick.

On the new ground, my mothers first cut the long grass with their hoes, bearing it off the field to be burned. They next dug and loosened the soil in places for the corn hills, which they laid off in rows. These hills they planted. Then all summer in this and other parts of the field they worked with their hoes, breaking and loosening the soil between the corn hills and cutting weeds.

Small trees and bushes, I know, were cut off with axes; but I remember little of this labor, most of it having been done the year before, when I was yet quite small. My father once told me that in very old times, when the women cleared a field, they first dug the corn hills with digging sticks, and afterwards worked between them with their bone hoes.

I remember this season's work the better for a dispute that my mothers had with two neighbors, Lone Woman and Goes-Back-to-Next-Timber. These two women were clearing lands that bordered our own. My father, I have said, to set up claim to our land, had placed boundary marks, one of them in the corner that touched the fields of Lone Woman and Goes-Back-to-Next-Timber. While my mothers were busy clearing and digging up the other end of their field, their two neighbors invaded this marked-off corner. Lone Woman had even dug up a small part before she was discovered.

My mothers showed Lone Woman the mark my father had placed. "This land belongs to us," they said; "but we will pay you and Goes-Back-to-Next-Timber for any rights you may think are yours. We do not want our neighbors to bear us any hard feelings."

We Indians thought our fields sacred, and we did not like to quarrel about them. A family's right to a field once having been set up, no one thought of disputing it. If any one tried to seize land belonging to another, we thought some evil would come upon him; as that one of his family would die or have some bad sickness.

There is a story of a hunter who had before been a black bear, and had been given great magic power. He dared try to catch eagles from another man's pit, and had his mind taken from him for doing so. Thus the gods punished him for entering ground that was not his own.

Lone Woman and Goes-Back-to-Next-Timber having withdrawn, my grandmother Turtle undertook to clear and break the ground that had been in dispute. She was a little woman but active, and she loved to work out-of-doors. Often, when my mothers were busy in the earth lodge, Turtle would go out to work in the field, and she would take me along for company. I was too little to help her any, but I liked to watch her work.

With her digging stick Turtle dug up a little round place in the center of the corner, and around this she circled from day to day, enlarging the dug-up space. She had folded her robe over her middle, like a pad. Resting the handle of her digging stick against her folded robe, she would drive the point into the soft earth to a depth equal to the length of my hand and pry up the soil.

She broke clods by striking them smartly with her digging stick. Roots of coarse grass, weeds, small brush and the like, she took in her hand and shook or struck them against the ground, to knock off the loose earth clinging to them. She then cast them into little piles to dry. In a few days she gathered these piles into a heap about four feet high and burned them.

My grandmother worked in this way all summer, but not always in the corner that had been in dispute. Some days, I remember, she dug along the edges of the field, to add to it and make the edges even. Of course, not all the labor of enlarging the field was done by Turtle; but she liked to have me with her when she worked, and I remember best what I saw her do.

It was my grandmother's habit to rise early in the summer months. She often arrived at the field before sunrise; about ten o'clock she returned to the lodge to eat and rest.

One morning, having come to the field quite early, I grew tired of my play before my grandmother had ended her work. "I want to go home," I begged, and I began to cry. Just then a strange bird flew into the field. It had a long curved beak, and made a queer cry, *cur-lew, cur-lew*.

I stopped weeping. My grandmother laughed.

"That is a curlew," she said. "Once at the mouth of the Knife river, a woman went out with her digging stick to dig wild turnips. The woman had a babe. Growing tired of carrying her babe on her back, she laid it on the ground.

"The babe began to cry. The mother was busy digging turnips, and did not go to her babe as she should have done. By and by she looked up. Her babe was flying away as a bird!

"The bird was a curlew, that cries like a babe. Now, if you cry, perhaps you, too, will turn into a curlew."

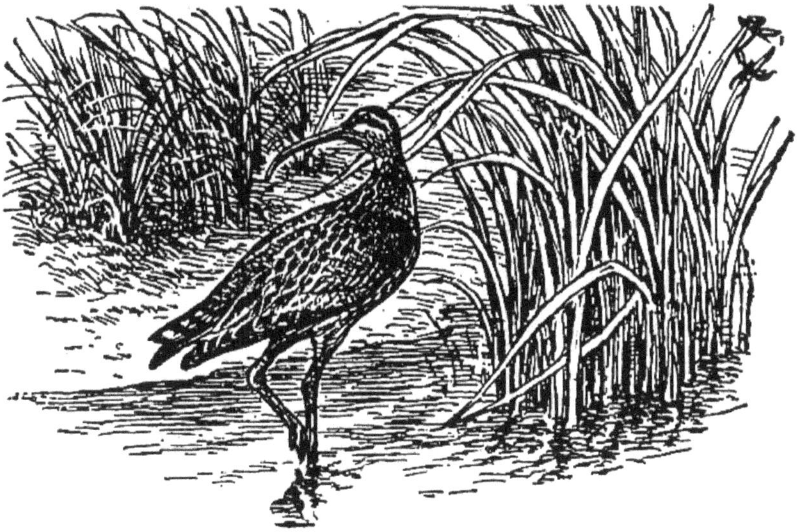

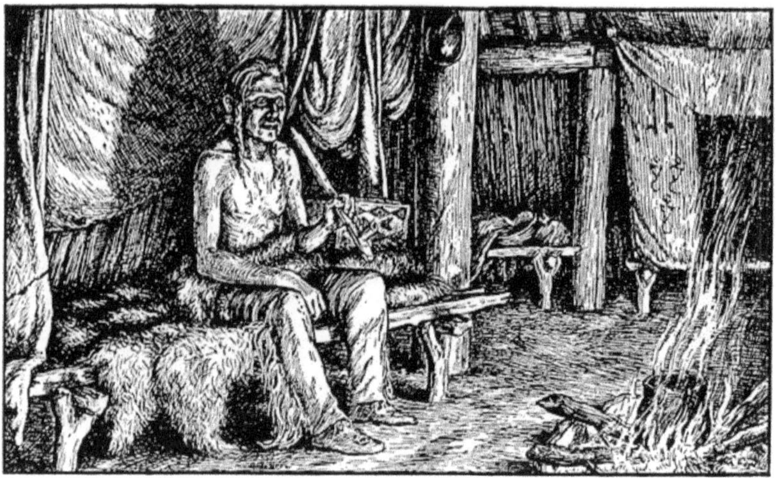

FIFTH CHAPTER

LIFE IN AN EARTH LODGE

The small lodges we built for winter did not stand long after we left them in the spring. Built on low ground by the Missouri, they were often swept away in the June rise; for in that month the river is flooded by snows melting in the Rocky Mountains.

The loss of our winter lodges never troubled us, however; for we thought of them as but huts. Then, too, we seldom wintered twice in the same place. We burned much firewood in our winter lodges, and before spring came the women had to go far to find it. The next season we made camp in a new place, where was plenty of dead-and-down wood for fuel.

We looked upon our summer lodges, to which we came every spring, as our real homes. There were about seventy of these, earth lodges well-built and roomy, in Like-a-Fishhook village. Most of them were built the second summer of our stay there.

My mothers' earth lodge—for the lodge belonged to the women of a household—was a large one, with floor measuring more than forty feet across. In the center was the fireplace. A screen of puncheons, set upright in a trench, stood between the fireplace and the door. This screen shut out draughts and kept out the dogs.

The screen ran quite to the sloping wall, on the right; but, on the left, there was space for a passage from the door to the fire. Right and left in an Indian lodge are reckoned as one stands at the fireplace, looking toward the door. We thought an earth lodge was alive and had a spirit like a human body, and that its front was like a face, with the door for mouth.

Before the fireplace and against the puncheon screen was my father's bed. Forked posts, eighteen inches high, stood in the earth floor. On poles laid in the forks rested cottonwood planks over which were thrown buffalo robes. A skin pillow, stuffed with antelope hair, lay at one end of the bed.

The beds of the rest of the family stood in the back of the lodge, against the wall. They were less simply made than my father's, being each covered with an old tent skin drawn over a frame of posts and poles. The bedding was of buffalo skins. As these could not be washed, my mothers used to take them out and hang them on the poles of the corn stage on sunny days, to air.

Most of the earth lodges—at least most of the larger ones—had each a bed like my father's before the fireplace; for this was the warmest place in the lodge. Usually the eldest in the family, as the father or grandfather, slept in this bed.

My father's bed, not being enclosed, made a good lounging place by day, and here he sat to smoke or chat with his friends. My mothers, too, used to sit here to peel wild turnips or make ready the daily meals.

Two or three sticks burned in the fireplace, not piled one upon the other as done by white men, but laid with ends meeting. As the ends burned away, the sticks were pushed in, keeping alive a small but hot fire. At night, the last thing my father did was to cover one of these burning sticks with ashes, that it might keep fire until morning.

Unless he had spent the night with some of his cronies, my father was the first to rise in the morning. He would go to the fireplace, draw out a buried coal, lay some dry sticks upon it, and blow with his breath until the fire caught. Sometimes he fanned the coal with a goose wing.

Soon a little column of smoke would rise toward the smoke hole, and my father would call, "Up, little daughter; up, sons! Get up, wives! The sun is up. To the river for your bath! Hasten!" And he would go up on the roof to look if enemies were about and if his horses were safe. My mothers were already up when I crept from my bed still sleepy, but glad that morning had come.

But if the weather was cold, we did not go to the river to bathe. An earthen pot full of water stood by one of the posts near the fire. It rested in a ring of bark, to keep it from falling. My mothers dipped each a big horn spoon full of water, filled her mouth, and, blowing the water over her palms, gave her face a good rubbing. Red Blossom washed my face in the same way. I did not like it very much, and I would shut my eyes and pucker my face when I felt the cold water. Red Blossom would say, "Why do you pucker up your face? You make it look like a piece of old, dried, buffalo skin."

Her face washed, Red Blossom sat on the edge of her bed and finished her toilet. She had a little fawn-skin bag, worked with red porcupine quills. From this bag she took her hairbrush, a porcupine tail mounted on a stick, with the sharp points of the quills cut off. She brushed her hair smooth, parting it in two braids that fell over each shoulder nearly hiding her ears. Red Blossom was no longer young, but her black tresses had not a grey hair in them.

She now opened her paint bag, put a little buffalo grease on her two fingers, pressed the tips lightly in the dry paint, and rubbed them over her cheeks and face. She also rubbed a little red into the part of her hair.

Meanwhile, the pot had been put on the fire. We Indians did not eat many things at a meal as white men do. Usually, breakfast was of one thing, often buffalo meat dried, and boiled to soften it. When a buffalo was killed, the meat was cut into thin slices, and some parts, into strips. These were dried in the open air over the earth lodge fire or in the smoke of a small fire out-of-doors. For breakfast, a round earthen pot was filled with water, dried meat put in, and the water brought to a boil. Red Blossom used to lift out the hot meat slices on the point of a stick, laying them on a bit of clean rawhide.

A rough bench stood back of the fireplace, a cottonwood plank, with ends resting on two blocks chopped from a tree trunk. My grandmother Turtle sat on this bench to eat her meals. My two mothers sat beside her, or on the floor near the meat they were serving. My father ate sitting on the edge of his couch. A wooden bowl, heaped with steaming meat, was set before each. Our fingers did for forks.

Boiling the meat in water made a thin broth which we used for a hot drink. It was very good, tasting much like white man's beef tea. We had no cups; but we had big spoons made of buffalo horn, and ladles, of mountain-sheep horn. Either of these did very well for drinking cups. Sometimes we used mussel shells.

A common breakfast dish was *mapee*[5] *naka-pah*,[6] or pounded-meal mush. From her cache pit Red Blossom took a string of dried squash slices. She cut off a length and tied the ends together, making a ring four or five inches in width. This ring and a double handful of beans she dropped in a pot of water, and set on the fire. When boiled, she lifted the ring out with a stick, with her horn ladle mashed the softened squash slices in a wooden bowl and put them back in the pot.

[5] mä pēē´

[6] nä kä päh´

Meanwhile Strikes-Many Woman or old Turtle had parched some corn in a clay pot, and toasted some buffalo fats on a stick, over the coals. Red Blossom now pounded the parched corn and toasted fats together in the corn mortar, and stirred the pounded mass into the pot with the squash and beans. The mess was soon done. Red Blossom dipped it into our bowls with a horn spoon.

We ate such messes with horn spoons or with mussel shells; for we Hidatsas had few metal spoons in those days. There was a shelf, or bench, at one side of the room, under the sloping roof, where were stored wooden bowls, uneaten foods, horn spoons, and the mussel shells that we used for teaspoons. When I was a little girl, nearly every family owned such shells, worn smooth and shiny from use.

After breakfast, unless it was in the corn season, when they went to the field, my mothers tidied up the lodge. They had short brooms of buckbrush. With these they swept the floor, stooping over and drawing the broom with a sidewise motion. As my father stabled his hunting ponies in the lodge at night, there was a good deal of litter to be taken out. Red Blossom used to scrape her sweepings into a skin basket, which she bore to the river bank and emptied.

Other tasks were then taken up; and there were plenty of them. Moccasins had to be made or old ones mended. Shirts and other garments had to be made. Often there were skins to be dressed or scraped. Leggings and shirts were embroidered usually in winter, when the women had no corn to hoe.

There was a good deal of visiting in our lodge; for my father was one of the chiefs of the village, and always kept open house. "If a man would be chief," we said, "he should be ready to feed the poor and strangers." A pot with buffalo meat or corn and beans cooking was always on the fire in my father's lodge. His friends and the other chief men of the village often came in to talk over affairs. A visitor came in without knocking, but did not sit down until he was asked.

Friends of my mothers also came in to sit and chat; and they often joined my mothers at whatever task they might be doing. Red Blossom would set a bowl of food before each. What she could not eat the guest took home with her. It was impolite to leave any uneaten food, as that would mean, "I do not like your cooking; it is unfit to eat."

My mothers were neat housekeepers and kept the ground about the lodge entrance swept as clean as the lodge floor; but many families were careless, and cast ashes, floor sweepings, scraps of broken bones and other litter on the ground about their lodges. In time this rubbish made little piles and became a nuisance, so that people could hardly walk in the paths between the lodges.

The Black Mouths then went through the village and ordered the women to clean up. The Black Mouths were a society of men of about forty years of age. They acted as police and punished any one who broke the camp laws.

These clean-ups were made rather often; in summer, perhaps twice a month. They were always ordered by the Black Mouths.

I remember one morning, just after breakfast, I heard singing, as of a dozen or more men coming toward our lodge. I started to run out to see what it was, but my mothers cried, "Do not go. It is the Black Mouths." My mothers, I thought, looked rather scared. We were still speaking, when I heard the tramp of feet. The door lifted, and the Black Mouths came in.

They looked very terrible, all painted with the lower half of the face black. Many, but not all, had the upper half of the face red. Some had eagles' feathers in their hair, and all wore robes or blankets. Some carried guns. Others had sticks about as long as my arm. With these sticks they beat any woman who would not help in the clean-up.

I fled to my father, but I dared not cry out, for I, too, was scared.

"One of you women go out and help clean up the village," said the Black Mouths. They spoke sternly, and several of them at once.

Like all the other women, my mothers were afraid of the Black Mouths "We will go," said both, and Red Blossom caught up broom and skin basket and went out.

The Black Mouths went also, and I followed to see what they did. They went into another lodge not far away. I heard voices, then the report of a gun, and a woman screamed. After a time, the Black Mouths came out driving before them a woman, very angry, but much frightened. She had not moved quickly enough to get her basket, and one of the Black Mouths had fired his gun at her feet to frighten her. The gun was loaded only with powder.

After they had made the rounds of the village, the Black Mouths returned to the lodge of their "keeper," a man named Crow Paunch. Soon we heard singing and drumming, and knew they were singing some of the society's songs.

When they had sung three or four times, there was silence for a while, as if a pipe were being passed. Then all came out and made the rounds a second time, to see if the work of cleaning was done and to hurry up the laggards. The village was all cleaned before noon; but some of the women got their work done sooner than others.

After the clean-up the village children came out to play in the spaces between the lodges, now swept clean and smooth. It was in these smooth spaces that the boys liked to play at throw sticks, light willow rods which they darted against the ground, whence they bounded to a great distance.

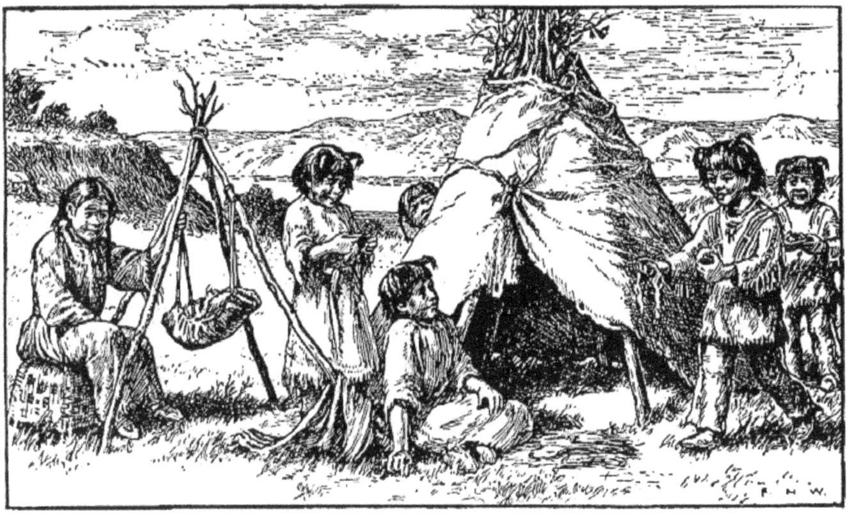

SIXTH CHAPTER

CHILDHOOD GAMES AND BELIEFS

White people seem to think that Indian children never have any play and never laugh. Such ideas seem very funny to me. How can any child grow up without play? I have seen children at our reservation school playing white men's games—baseball, prisoners' base, marbles. We Indian children also had games. I think they were better than white children's games.

I look back upon my girlhood as the happiest time of my life. How I should like to see all my little girl playmates again! Some still live, and when we meet at feasts or at Fourth-of-July camp, we talk of the good times we had when we were children.

My little half sister was my usual playmate. She was two years younger than I, and I loved her dearly. She had a pretty name, Cold Medicine. On our prairies grows a flower with long, yellow root. In old times, if a warrior was running from enemies and became wearied he chewed a bit of the root and rubbed it on his eyelids. It made his eyes and tongue feel cold and kept him awake. The flower for this reason was called cold medicine. When my father spoke my sister's name, it made him think of this flower and of the many times he had bravely gone out with war parties.

For playgrounds my little sister and I had the level spaces between the lodges or the ground under the corn stage, in sunny weather; and the big, roomy floor of the earth lodge, if it rained or the weather were chill. We liked, too, to play in the lodge in the hot days of the Cherry moon; for it was cool inside, never hot and stuffy like a white man's house. In the fall, when the air was frosty, the sun often shone, and we could play in the big yellow sunspot that fell on the floor through the smoke hole.

We liked to play at housekeeping, especially in the warm spring days, when we had returned from winter camp and could again play out-ofdoors. With the help of the neighbors' children, we fetched long forked sticks. These we stacked like a tepee frame and covered with robes that we borrowed. To this play tent we brought foods and had a feast.

Sometimes little boys joined in our play; and then it was like real housekeeping. We girls chose each a little boy for husband. To my little husband I said, "Old man, get your arrows, and go kill some buffaloes. We are hungry. Go at once!"

My little husband hastened to his mother and told her our needs. She laughed and gave him a boiled buffalo tongue; or perhaps pemmican, dried meat pounded fine and mixed with marrow fat. This and the foods which the other little husbands fetched us, we girls laid on fresh, clean grass that we pulled. Then we sat down to feast, the little girls on one side of the fireplace, the little boys on the other, just as we had seen men and women sit when they feasted. Only there really was no fireplace. We just made believe there was.

In summer, my little sister and I often went to the river for wet clay, which we modeled into figures. There is a smooth, blue clay found in places at the water's edge, very good for modeling. We liked best to make human figures, man, woman, or little child. We dried them in the shade, else the sun cracked them. I fear they were not very beautiful. When we made a mud man, we had to give him three legs to make him stand up.

I had a doll, woven of rushes, that Turtle made me. It really was not a doll, but a cradle, such as Indian women used for carrying a small child. In winter I had my deer-skin doll, with the beads for eyes. My grandmother had made me a little bed for my dolls. The frame was of willows, and it was covered with gopher skins, tanned and sewed together. In this little bed my sister and I used to put our dollies to sleep.

We had a game of ball much like shinny. It was a woman's game, but we little girls played it with hooked sticks. We also had a big, soft ball, stuffed with antelope hair, which we would bounce in the air with the foot. The game was to see how long a girl could bounce the ball without letting it touch the ground. Some girls could bounce it more than a hundred times. It was lots of fun.

We coasted in winter, on small sleds made of buffalo ribs; but coasting on the snow was rather for boys and older girls. There was another kind of coaster that we girls liked. A buffalo skin has the hair lying backwards, towards the flanks. I would borrow a skin of my mothers and tie a thong through two of the stake holes at the head or neck, to draw it by. Such a skin made a good coaster even in summer on a steep hillside; for, laid head forward, it slid smoothly over the soft grass.

Girls of thirteen or fourteen were fond of playing at "tossing in a blanket," or "foot-moving," as we called it. There were fifteen or twenty players. A newly dried skin was borrowed, one that was scraped clean of hair. There were always holes cut in the edges of a hide, to stake it to the ground while drying. Into each hole a small hard wood stick was now thrust and twisted around, for a handle.

Along the ditch at the edge of the village grew many tall weeds. The players pulled armfuls of these and made them into a pile. They laid the hide on this pile of weeds; and, with a player at every one of the stick handles, they stretched the hide taut.

A girl now lay downward on the hide. With a quick pull, the others tossed her into the air, when she was expected to come down on her feet, to be instantly tossed again. The game was to see how many times she could be tossed without falling. A player was often tossed ten or more times before she lost her balance. Each time, as she came down, she kept turning in one direction, right or left. When at last she fell, the pile of weeds saved her from any hurt.

We called the game *eetseepadahpakee*,[7] or foot-moving, from the player's habit of wriggling her feet when in the air. We thought this wriggling, or foot moving, a mark of skill.

[7] ēēt sēē pä däh´ pä kēē

But, if my mothers let me play much of the time, they did not forget to teach me good morals. "We are a family that has not a bad woman in it," they used to say. "You must try hard not to be naughty."

My grandfather Big Cloud often talked to me. "My granddaughter," he would say, "try to be good, so that you will grow up to be a good woman. Do not quarrel nor steal. Do not answer anyone with bad words. Obey your parents, and remember all that I say."

When I was naughty my mothers usually scolded me; for they were kind women and did not like to have me punished. Sometimes they scared me into being good, by saying, "The owl will get you." This saying had to do with an old custom that I will explain.

Until I was about nine years old, my hair was cut short, with a tuft on either side of my head, like the horns of an owl. Turtle used to cut my hair. She used a big, steel knife. In old times, I have heard, a thin blade of flint was used. I did not like Turtle's hair cutting a bit, because she *pulled*.

"Why do you cut my hair, grandmother?" I asked.

"It is our custom," Turtle answered. "I will tell you the story."

"Thousands and thousands of years ago, there lived a great owl. He was strong and had magic power, but he was a bad bird. When the hunters killed buffaloes, the owl would turn all the meat bitter, so that the Indians could not eat it, and so they were always hungry.

"On this earth then lived a young man called the Sun's Child; for the sun was his father. He heard how the Indians were made hungry, and came to help them.

"The owl lived in a hollow tree that had a hole high up in its trunk. The Sun's Child climbed the tree, and when the owl put his head out of the hole, he caught the bird by the neck.

"'Do not let the Sun's Child kill me!' the owl cried to the Indians. 'I have been a bad bird; now I will be good and I will help your children.

"'As soon as a child is old enough to understand you when you speak to him, cut his hair with two tufts like my own. Do this to make him look like an owl; and I will remember and make the child grow up strong and healthy. If a child weeps or will not obey, say to him, "The owl will get you!" This will frighten him, so that he will obey you.'"

Plate I.—Offering food before the shrine of the Big Birds' ceremony

It was thus my mothers frightened me when I was naughty. Red Blossom would call, "O owl, I have a bad daughter. Come."

"I will be good, I will be good!" I would cry, as I ran to my father. I knew he would not let the owl hurt me.

My old grandfather, Missouri River, taught me of the gods. He was a medicine man and very holy, and I was rather afraid of him. He used to sit on the bench behind the fire, to smoke. He had a long pipe, of polished black stone. He liked best to smoke dried tobacco blossoms which he first oiled with buffalo fat.

One day, as he sat smoking, I asked him, "Grandfather, who are the gods?"

Missouri River took a long pull at his pipe, blew the smoke from his nostrils, and put the stem from his mouth. "Little granddaughter," he answered, "this earth is alive and has a soul or spirit, just as you have a spirit. Other things also have spirits, the sun, clouds, trees, beasts, birds. These spirits are our gods. We pray to them and offer them food, that they may help us when we have need."

"Do the spirits eat the food?" I asked. I had seen my grandfather set food before the two skulls of the Big Birds' ceremony.

"No," said my grandfather, "They eat the food's spirit; for the food has a spirit as have all things. When the gods have eaten of its spirit, we often take back the food to eat ourselves."

"How do we know there are gods, grandfather?" I asked.

"They appear to us in our dreams. That is why the medicine man fasts and cuts his flesh with knives. If he fasts long, he will fall in a vision. In this vision the gods will come and talk with him."

"What are the gods like?" I asked.

"Like beings that live on this earth. Some are as men. Others are as birds, or beasts, or even plants and other things. Not all the gods are good. Some seek to harm us. The good gods send us buffaloes, and rain to make our corn grow."

"Do they send us thunder?" I asked. There had been a heavy storm the day before.

"The thunder bird god sends us thunder," said my grandfather. "He is like a great swallow, with wings that spread out like clouds. Lightning is the flash of his eyes. His scream makes the thunder."

"Once in Five Villages," my grandfather went on, "there lived a brave man who owned a gun. One day a storm blew up. As the man sat in his lodge, there came a clap of thunder and lightning struck his roof, tearing a great hole.

"This did not frighten the man at all. Indeed, it angered him. He caught up his gun and fired it through the hole straight into the sky. 'You thunder bird,' he shouted, 'stay away from my lodge. See this gun. If you come, I will shoot at you again!'"

My grandfather paused to fill his pipe. "That was a brave man," he said as he reached for a coal. "Perhaps the thunder bird loves brave men, and did not harm him. But it is not well to provoke the gods. My little granddaughter should never laugh at them nor speak of them lightly."

My grandfather spoke very solemnly.

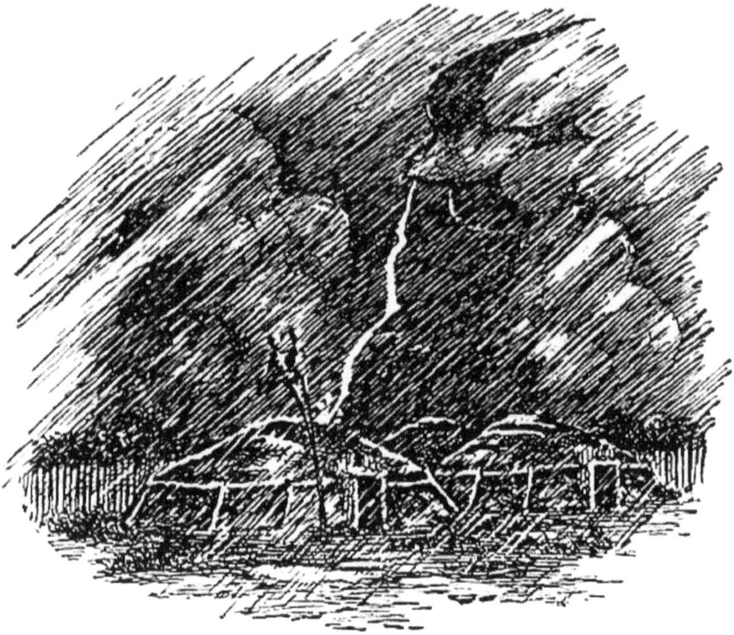

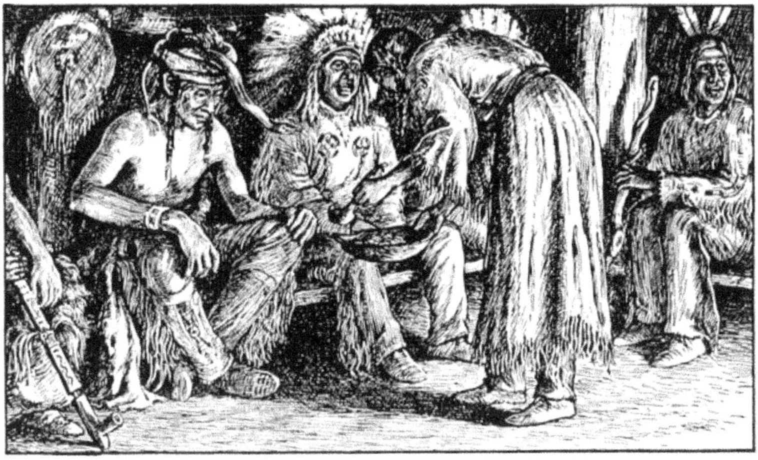

SEVENTH CHAPTER

KINSHIP, CLAN COUSINS

We Hidatsas do not reckon our kin as white men do. If a white man marries, his wife is called by his name; and his children also, as Tom Smith, Mary Smith. We Indians had no family names. Every Hidatsa belonged to a clan; but a child, when he was born, became a member of his mother's, not his father's clan.

An Indian calls all members of his clan his brothers and sisters. The men of his father's clan he calls his clan fathers; and the women, his clan aunts. Thus I was born a member of the *Tsistska*[8], or Prairie Chicken clan, because my mother was a *Tsistska*. My father was a member of the *Meedeepahdee*,[9] or Rising Water clan. Members of the *Tsistska* clan are my brothers and sisters; but my father's clan brothers, men of the *Meedeepahdee*, are my clan fathers, and his clan sisters are my clan aunts.

[8] Tsïst´ skä

[9] Mēē dēē päh´ dēē

These relations meant much to us Indians. Members of a clan were bound to help one another in need, and thought the gods would punish them if they did not. Thus, if my mother was in need, members of the *Tsistska* clan helped her. If she was hungry, they gave her food. If her child was naughty, my mother called in a *Meedeepahdee* to punish him, a clan father, if the child was a boy; if a girl, a clan aunt; for parents did not punish their own children. Again, when my father died, his clan fathers and clan aunts it was, who bore him to the burial scaffold and prayed his ghost not to come back to trouble the villagers.

Another clan relative is *makutsatee*,[10] or clan cousin. I reckon as my clan cousins all members of my tribe whose fathers are my clan fathers. Thus, my mother, I have said, was a Prairie Chicken; my father, a member of the *Meedeepahdee*, or Rising Water, clan. Another woman, of what clan does not matter, is also married to a *Meedeepahdee*; her children will be my clan cousins, because their father, being a *Meedeepahdee*, is my clan father.

[10] mä kut´ sä tēē

Clan cousins had a custom that will seem strange to white people. We Indians are proud, and it makes our hearts sore if others make mock of us. In olden times if a man said to his friend, even in jest, "You are like a dog," his friend would draw his knife to fight. I think we Indians are more careful of our words than white men are.

But it is never good for a man not to know his faults, and so we let one's clan cousins tease him for any fault he had. Especially was this teasing common between young men and young women. Thus a young man might be unlucky in war. As he passed the fields where the village women hoed their corn, he would hear some mischievous girl, his clan cousin, singing a song taunting him for his ill success. Were any one else to do this, the young man would be ready to fight; but, seeing that the singer was his clan cousin, he would laugh and call out, "Sing louder cousin, sing louder, that I may hear you."

I can best explain this custom by telling you a story:

Story of Snake Head-Ornament

A long time ago, in one of our villages at Knife river, lived a man named *Mapuksaokihe*,[11] or Snake Head-Ornament. He was a great medicine man.

In a hole in the floor of his earth lodge, there lived a bull snake. Snake Head-Ornament called the bull snake "father."

[11] Mä pu̱k´ sä ō kēē hĕ

When Snake Head-Ornament was invited to a feast, he would paint his face, wrap himself in his best robe and say, "Come, father; let us go and get something to eat."

The bull snake would creep from his hole, crawl up the man's body and coil about his neck, thrusting his head over the man's forehead; or he would coil about the man's head like the headcloth of a hunter, with his head thrust forward, as I have said.

Bearing the snake thus on his head, Snake Head-Ornament would enter the lodge where the feast was held and sit down to eat. The snake, however, did not eat of the food that Snake Head-Ornament ate. The snake's food was scrapings of buffalo hides that the women of the lodge fed him.

When Snake Head-Ornament came home, he would say to the bull snake, "Father, get off." And the snake would crawl down the man's body and into his den again.

Snake Head-Ornament fasted and had a vision. In the vision his gods, he thought, bade him go to war. He made up a war party and led it against enemies on the Yellowstone river. The party not only killed no enemies, but lost three of their own men; and they thought Snake Head-Ornament was to blame for it. "You said your prayers were strong," they said; "and we have lost three men! Your gods have not helped us."

Snake Head-Ornament thought his gods were angry with him; and when he came home he went about crying and mourning and calling upon his gods to give him another vision. "Pity me, gods," he cried, "make me strong that I may bring home scalps and horses." He was a brave man, and his bad fortune made his heart sore.

In those days, when a man mourned he cut off his hair, painted his body with white clay, and threw away his moccasins. He also cut his flesh with a knife or some sharp weapon. Now when a man sought a vision from the gods, he wept and mourned, that the gods might have pity on him; and for this he went away from the village, alone, into the hills. So it happened, that Snake Head-Ornament, on his way to the hills, went mourning and crying past a field where sat a woman, his clan cousin, on her watch-stage. Seeing him, she began a song to tease him:

He said, "I am a young bird!"

If a young bird, he should be in his nest;

But he comes here looking gray,

And wanders about outside the village!

He said, "I am a young snake!"

If a young snake, he should be in the hills among the red buttes;

But he comes here looking gray and crying,

And wanders aimlessly about!

When the woman sang, "He comes here looking gray," she meant that the man was gray from the white-clay paint on his body.

Snake Head-Ornament heard her song; but, knowing she was his clan sister, he cried out to her: "Sing louder, cousin! You are right; let my 'fathers' hear what you say. I do not know if they will feel shame or not, but the bull snake and the bald eagle both called me 'son'!"

What he meant was that the bull snake and the bald eagle were his dream gods. That is, they had appeared to him in a dream, and promised to help him as they would a son, when he went to war. In her song, the woman taunted him with this. If she had not been his clan cousin, he would have been beside himself with anger. As it was, he but laughed and did not hurt her.

But the woman had cause for singing her song. Years before, when Snake Head-Ornament was a very young man, he went out with a war party and killed a Sioux woman. When he came home the people called him brave, and made much of him; and he grew quite puffed up now that all looked up to him.

Not long after, he was made a member of the Black Mouth society. It happened one day, that the women were building a fence of logs, set upright around the village, to defend it from enemies. Snake Head-Ornament, as a member of the Black Mouths, was one of the men overseeing the work. This woman, his clan cousin, was slow at her task; and, to make her move more briskly, Snake Head-Ornament came close to her and fired off his gun just past her knees. She screamed, but seeing it was Snake Head-Ornament who had shot, and knowing he was her clan cousin, she did not get angry. Nevertheless, she did not forget! And, years after, she had revenge in her taunting song.

Young men going out with a war party had to take much chaffing from older warriors who were clan cousins. My brother was once out with a party of fifty, many of them young men. They were fleeing from a big camp of Sioux and had ridden for two days. The second night one of the younger men, a mere lad, fell asleep as he rode his pony. An older warrior, his clan cousin, fired a gun past the lad's ear. "Young man," he cried, "you sleep so soundly that only thunder can waken you!" The rest of the party thought the warrior's words a huge joke.

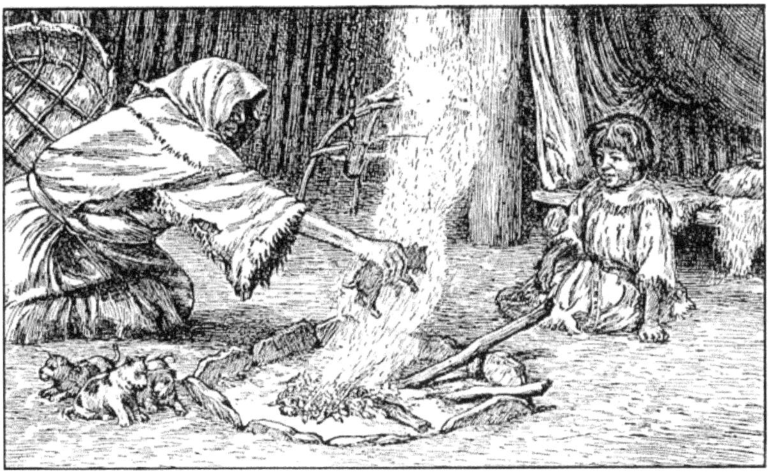

EIGHTH CHAPTER

INDIAN DOGS

In old times we Indian people had no horses, and not many families of my tribe owned them when I was a little girl. But I do not think there ever was a time when we Hidatsas did not own dogs. We trained them to draw our tent poles and our loaded travois. We never used dogs to chase deer, as white men do.

Our Hidatsa dogs—the breed we owned when I was a little girl—had broad faces, with gentle, knowing eyes; erect, pointed ears; and tails curling, never trailing like a wolf's tail. They had soft silky hair, gray, black, or spotted red or white. All had stout, heavy legs. I think this sturdiness was because we saved only dogs of stout build to drag our travois.

The Teton Sioux, who lived south of us, owned dogs like ours, but of slenderer build and legs. They liked these dogs, I think, because they were speedier; for the Sioux were hunters, always moving from place to place.

Almost every family in Like-a-Fishhook village owned two or more dogs; and, as there were about seventy lodges in the village, our dogs made a large pack. The dogs knew every man and child in the village, and being, besides, well trained, seldom bit anyone. But they were quick to wind a stranger. A visitor from another tribe was sure to be beset by a troop of dogs, growling and barking at his heels.

The dogs had one habit I liked. Every evening about bedtime—and bedtime for a little Indian girl was early—some dog was sure to start up, *wu-wu-wu!* And all the others would join in, even the little puppies. I used to lie in my bed and listen to them.

About midnight, the barking would start up again, especially if there was a moon, and again a little before daylight; but I was usually asleep at these hours.

In daytime lookouts were always on the roofs of some of the lodges watching if enemies or buffaloes were about. If they saw our hunters, with meat, coming home over the prairie, these lookouts would cry out, "*Hey-da-ey!*"[12] And the dogs, knowing what the cry meant, would join in with "*wu-u-u-u.*"[13] They liked fresh buffalo meat no less than the Indians.

[12] Hey dä ey´

[13] Wu-u-u

But the greatest excitement was when enemies were seen. The lookouts then cried, "*Ahahuts*[14]—*they come against us!*" Warriors, on hearing the cry, seized weapons and ran out of their lodges, yelling shrilly. The chiefs sprang for their ponies, twisting lariats into the ponies' mouths for bridles. Medicine men chanted holy songs, and women ran about calling to their children. But above all rose the barking of the dogs, every beast joining in the hubbub.

[14] A hä huts´

One day, after the midday meal—I think I was then eight years old—old Turtle went down to the river and fetched an armful of dry willows. They were about four feet long and as thick as a child's wrist; some were forked at the top. She set them in a circle, with tops together like a tepee, at one side of the lodge entrance near the place where the dogs slept.

"What are you doing, grandmother?" I asked.

Turtle did not answer my question. "I want to get some dry grass," she said. "Come and help me."

We went out to a place in the hills where was some long, dead grass. Turtle pulled a big armful, piling it on her robe which she spread on the ground. She drew the corners of the robe together, slung the bundle over her shoulder and we came back to the village.

She laid the grass thickly over the sides of the little tepee, leaning chunks of wood against it to keep the grass in place. She left a door, or opening, in front; and she even bound a stick over the door, like the pole over the door of a hunting lodge. Last, she put grass inside, as if for a bed.

"Grandmother, what *are* you doing?" I begged; but she led me into the lodge, telling me nothing.

I was awakened early the next morning by dogs barking on the roof. As I lay listening, I thought I heard a faint whining outside. It seemed to come from the place where the little grass tepee stood.

I fell asleep, and awoke a second time to see Red Blossom fanning the fire with a goose wing. Breakfast was soon ready, of fresh boiled buffalo meat. The hunters had come in only the night before, and they had brought a fresh side-and-ribs for a present to my father.

After the meal I saw Turtle gather up the scraps of meat into a wooden bowl. "Come," she said, leading me out of the lodge.

She stopped before the tepee, and thrust the bowl of scraps within. Again I heard the faint whining. I dropped to my knees and looked in. There I saw our best dog, the pet of us all; and beside her lay four little puppies.

"*Eh, sukkeets!*"[15] I cried, "Oh, good!" And I drew the puppies out one by one, to cuddle them. The mother dog whined, and raised her eyes to me. She was a gentle dog and did not snap at my hand.

[15] sŭk´ kēēts

I do not know whether I or the puppies' mother cuddled them more, the next few days. One puppy I came to love dearly. He was a wriggling little thing, with a bob tail for all the world like a rabbit's, except that it hung down. There were ten or more bobtailed dogs in the village all of them born so. My puppy was black, so I named him *Sheepeesha*,[16] or Blackie.

[16] Shēē´ pēē shä

It must have been a funny sight to see me take my puppy out for a walk. Stooping, I would lay the puppy between my shoulders and draw my tiny robe up over his back; and I would walk off proud as any Indian mother of her new babe. The old mother dog would creep half out of her kennel, following me with her gentle eyes. I was careful not to go out of her sight.

When the puppies were ten days old my grandmother brought in some fresh sage, the kind we Indians use in a sweat lodge. She laid the sage by the fireplace and fetched in the puppies, barring the door so that the mother dog could not come in. I could hear the poor dog whining pitifully.

"What are you going to do, grandmother?" I asked.

"I am going to smoke the puppies."

"Why, grandmother?" I cried.

"Because the puppies are old enough to eat cooked meat, for their teeth have come through. The sage is a sacred plant. Its smoke will make the puppies hungry, so that they will eat."

While she was speaking, she opened my little pet's jaws. Sure enough, four white teeth were coming through the gums.

Turtle raked some coals from the ashes, and laid on them a handful of the sage. A column of thick white smoke arose upward to the smoke hole.

My grandmother took my puppy in her hands and held his head in the smoke. The poor puppy struggled and choked. Thick spittle, like suds, came out of his mouth. I was frightened, and thought he was going to die.

"The smoke will make the puppy healthy," said Turtle. "Now let us see if he will grow up strong, to carry my little granddaughter's tent."

She lifted the puppy, still choking, from the floor, and let him fall so that he landed on his feet. The puppy was still young and weak, and he was strangling; but his little legs stiffened, and he stood without falling.

"Hey, hey," laughed my grandmother. "This is a strong dog! He will grow up to carry your tent." For in old times, when traveling, we Hidatsas made our dogs drag our tents on poles, like travois.

Turtle tried the other three puppies. One, not as strong as the rest, fell on his side. "This dog will not grow up strong," said my grandmother. "I will give him to my neighbor, who asks for one."

She now lifted a clay pot out of the ashes, and from it poured something into a flat bowl; corn mush, I think it was, boiled with buffalo fats. She set the bowl before the puppies. They quickly lapped up the mush, with funny red tongues. My little black puppy even gulped down a lump of fat.

Turtle laughed. "I told you your puppy is strong," she cried. "He will soon grow up to carry your tent. But to grow, our puppies must be fed. It will be your work to feed them. See they do not starve."

But, if I had to feed the puppies, my grandmother also helped. Indeed, the whole family watched to see that they had enough. If fresh meat was brought in, we always boiled some and gave to the puppies. We did not give them raw meat. "It is not good for puppies. It will make them sick," said Turtle.

But, as the puppies grew up, we began to feed them raw meat. My grandmother sometimes boiled corn for them, into a coarse mush. They were fond of this. As they grew older, any food that turned sour or was unfit for the family to eat was given me for my doggies. They ate it greedily. It did not seem to harm them.

Sometimes a deer or elk was killed, that was poor in flesh. Such a carcass was cut up and given to the dogs of the village, and of course mine got their share.

When several buffaloes were killed, the hunters often could not carry all the meat home, and took only the best cuts. The next day any one who wanted, could go out and take the cast-away pieces for her dogs. Then, there were parts that we always threw away or gave to the dogs. The tough, outside meat of a buffalo's hams we cut off and saved for the dogs. The inside meat, next the bone, we thought our very best. Hunters were fond of roasting it before the fire, on two stones.

Even in famine times we did not forget our dogs; but we sometimes had only soft bones to give them that had been broken for boiling. The dogs gnawed these, and so got a little food.

We Hidatsas loved our good dogs, and were kind to them.

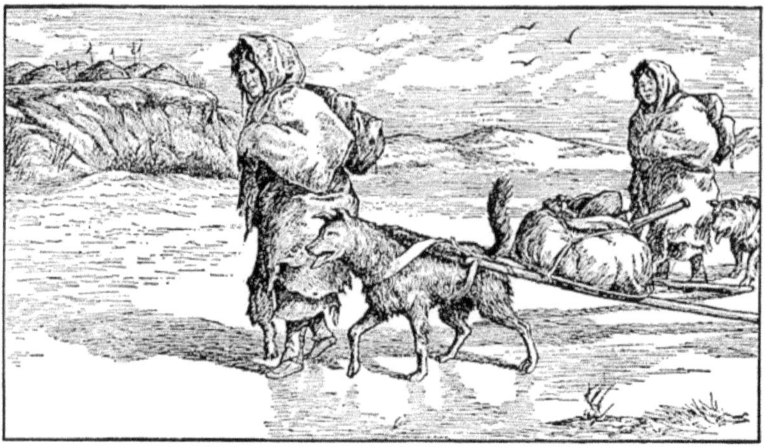

NINTH CHAPTER

TRAINING A DOG

Autumn twice came around, and my puppy had grown into a romping dog. In the moon of Yellow Leaves, my tribe went again into winter camp. We returned to Like-a-Fishhook village rather early in the spring. Patches of snow lay on the ground, and the ice was still firm on the Missouri when we crossed. We reached the village in midafternoon.

My father had two pack horses loaded with our stuff and our dogs dragged well-laden travois. While my mothers were unpacking, my father made a fire. He drew his flint and steel, and with a bit of soft, rotten wood for tinder struck a spark. In olden times the Hidatsas made fire with two sticks. "I saw very old men make fire thus, when I was a lad," my grandfather once told me. I never saw it done myself.

Small Ankle wrapped the spark, caught in the tinder, in a little bunch of dry grass, and waved it in the air until the grass was ablaze. He had raked together some bits of charcoal in the fireplace and on them laid a few dry-wood splinters. To these he held the burning grass and soon had a fire.

There was a little firewood in the lodge, left from the previous autumn, but not enough to keep the fire going long. As my mothers were still unpacking, my father offered to go out and get wood for the night. Getting wood, we thought, was woman's work; but my father was a kind man, willing to help his wives.

From the saddle of one of his horses Small Ankle took a rawhide lariat, and to one end fastened a short stick. There were some cottonwoods under the river bank, not far from the village. Into one of the largest trees Small Ankle threw his lariat until the stick caught in some dead branches overhead. A sharp pull broke off the branches. My father gathered them up and bore them to the lodge.

There were logs and dead wood lying along the river, but they were wet with the snows. My father knew the dead branches in the trees would be dried by the winds. He wanted dry wood to kindle a quick fire.

The next morning after we had eaten, Red Blossom took her ax, and, dragging a travois from its place against the fire screen, led the way out of the lodge. Strikes-Many Woman followed her. Our biggest dog, lying outside, saw them coming. He got up, shaking himself, wagging his tail, and barking *wu-wu-wu!* Our dogs were always ready to be harnessed. They liked to go to the woods, knowing they would be fed well afterwards.

This, our best dog, was named *Akeekahee*,[17] or Took-from-Him. He belonged to Red Blossom. A woman owning a dog would ask some brave man of her family to name him for her; and Red Blossom had asked my grandfather, Big Cloud, to name her dog. Once an enemy had stolen his horse, but Big Cloud gave chase and retook his horse from that bad enemy. For this, he named the dog Took-from-Him.

[17] kēē´ kä hēē

My mothers harnessed their dogs, four in number and started off. They returned a little after midday; first, Red Blossom, with a great pack of wood on her back; after her, Strikes-Many Woman; then the four dogs, marching one behind the other, Took-from-Him in the lead. Each dog dragged a travois loaded with wood.

My mothers dropped their loads before the lodge entrance. The dogs were unhitched; and, while old Turtle fed them, Strikes-Many Woman carried the wood into the lodge and piled it by the corral, where it was handy to the fire.

I was eager to have my dog broken to harness and begged my grandmother to make a travois for him. "I will," she said, "but wait another moon. Your dog will then be fed fat, after the long winter. A dog should be two years old, and strong, when he is broken. To work a dog too young or when he is weak will hurt his back."

A month after this, my mothers came home one afternoon from woodgathering, dragging each a cottonwood pole about eight feet long. They peeled these poles bare of bark, and laid them up on the corn stage to dry.

"What are the poles for?" I asked.

"They are for your travois," said my grandmother. "Your dog *Sheepeesha* is now old enough to work; and my little granddaughter, too, must learn to be useful."

I was ready to cry out and dance, when I heard these words of my grandmother; and I thought I could never, never wait until those poles dried. The heavy ladder we used for mounting the stage lay on the ground when not in use. I was too little to lift it, to climb up to the poles; but I went every day to stand below and gaze at them longingly.

One afternoon my grandmother fetched the poles into the lodge. "They are dry now," she said. "I will make the travois frame."

With her big knife she hacked the greater ends of the poles flat, so that they would run smooth on the ground. The small ends she crossed for the joint, cutting a notch in each to make them fit. She bound the joint with strips of the big tendon in a buffalo's neck that we Indians call the *eetsuta*[18]. These strips drew taut as they dried, making the joint firm.

[18] ēēt sụ´ tä

Turtle now drew a saddle, or cushion, over the poles just under the joint, sewing it down with buckskin thongs. This saddle was to keep the dog from fretting his shoulders against the poles.

The hoop for the basket was of ash. My father webbed it. He cut a long, thin thong from the edges of a hide, and soaked it to make it soft. Taking some wet paint in his palm, he drew the thong through it, thus painting it a bright red. He laced the thong over the hoop and my grandmother bound the basket in place.

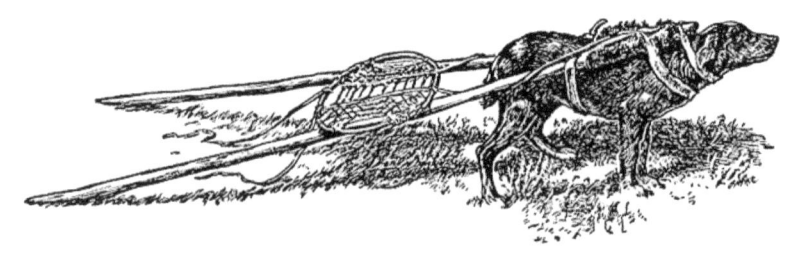

The harness was of two pieces: a collar, to go around the dog's neck; and a breast thong, that was drawn across his chest and through a loop in the saddle, was lapped once or twice around one of the travois poles, and was finally carried under the dog's body to the other pole, where it was made fast.

I could hardly wait to eat my breakfast the next morning, for my mothers had promised to take me with them to gather wood. "And we are going to begin training your dog to-day," they told me.

I knew a dog should be fed before he was harnessed, and I saved half my breakfast meat to give to mine. Owning a dog, and invited to go with my mothers to get wood, I felt that in spite of my girlish years I was almost a woman now.

Breakfast ended, Red Blossom fetched the new travois and laid it on my dog's back. He looked up, puzzled, then sank to the ground and lay wagging his tail from side to side, sweeping a clean place in the dust. Red Blossom bound the collar about his neck, and drew and fastened the breast thong. While she was doing this I gently patted my dog's head.

"*Nah!*" said Red Blossom, "Come!" But my doggie was a bit frightened. He twisted about, trying to rid himself of the travois, but only hurt himself. He looked up at me and whined. Red Blossom tied a thong to his collar and put the end in my hand. "Lead him," she said. "He will follow the other dogs." She led off, Strikes-Many Woman behind her, and the dogs followed after, in a line.

I tugged at my dog's thong, pursing my lips and making a whistling sound, as Indians do. My doggie understood. He rose to his feet, and, seeing the other dogs moving off, followed after the last one.

We thus came to the woods, about a mile and a half from the village. The dogs sank in their tracks, to rest. My mothers searched about for dead-and-dry wood, which they cut into lengths of two feet or more, and piled them in the path near the dogs.

When they had enough wood cut, my mothers lifted each travois by its basket, and turned it so that the dog's nose was pointed toward the village; and they loaded each travois with a double armful of wood, bound to the basket with two thongs. My two mothers then lifted each a load to her own back, and started to the village.

I did not carry any load myself, as my shoulders were not strong enough for such heavy work; but I led my dog. Not a very big load was put on him, as it was his first. I called to him, tugging gently at the thong. Seeing the other dogs ahead, he followed willingly.

Old Turtle awaited us at the door. "Grandmother," I cried joyfully, "my dog has brought home a load of wood. He did not try to run away." Turtle laughed, and helped me unload.

That evening I was sitting by the fire with my good dog, for Red Blossom had let me bring him into the lodge. Now and then I slipped him a bit of meat I had saved from my supper. My father had laid some dry sticks on the fire, and the blaze flickered and rose, flickered and rose, making post and rafter yellow with its light. Small Ankle sat on his couch smoking his pipe. Suddenly I heard the clitter of the hollow hoofs as the lodge door was raised and let fall again. I looked up. Coyote Eyes, a Ree Indian, was coming around the screen.

"*Hau!*"[19] cried my father, making a place for him on the couch. Small Ankle was a polite man. He handed his pipe to the Ree, who took big pulls, blowing the smoke through his nostrils.

[19] Hau (How)

Coyote Eyes gave the pipe back to my father. "That is a fine dog you have," he said to me. "I know a story of my tribe about two dogs."

Being but a little girl, I did not think it proper for me to talk to a stranger, but my father answered for me, "What is the story?"

"In the beginning, my tribe came out of a cave in the earth," said Coyote Eyes. "They journeyed until they came to the Missouri river. 'Let us go up this river,' they said, 'and find a place to build our villages.' They were weary of journeying.

"They had two dogs in the camp. One was black; his name was Death. The other was white, and her name was Sickness. These dogs were asleep when the tribe broke camp the next morning. The people were in such haste to be off that they forgot to waken the dogs.

"The third day after, they saw two great fires sweeping toward them over the prairie. The women cried out with fear. All thought that they should die.

"When the fires came near, the people saw that they were the two dogs, Death and Sickness.

"'Do not fear,' said the dogs. 'Our hearts are not all evil. True, we will bite you, because you forgot us; but we will also live with you and be your friends. We will carry your burdens; and when we die, you shall eat us.'

"The dogs grew old. The white one died, and her skin became the squash. Now our squashes are of different colors, white, gray, yellow, spotted, just as are dogs. These squashes we eat. Also we Rees eat dog meat; for, before he died, the black dog said, 'You shall eat my flesh.'

"And to this day, when our Ree people sicken and die, they say, 'We are bitten by Sickness and Death.'"

My father smiled. "We Hidatsas do not eat dogs," he said; and then to me, "Little daughter, it is bedtime."

I did not always obey my mothers; for, like all little girls, I was naughty sometimes, but I dared not disobey my father.

I put my dog out of the lodge, and went to bed.

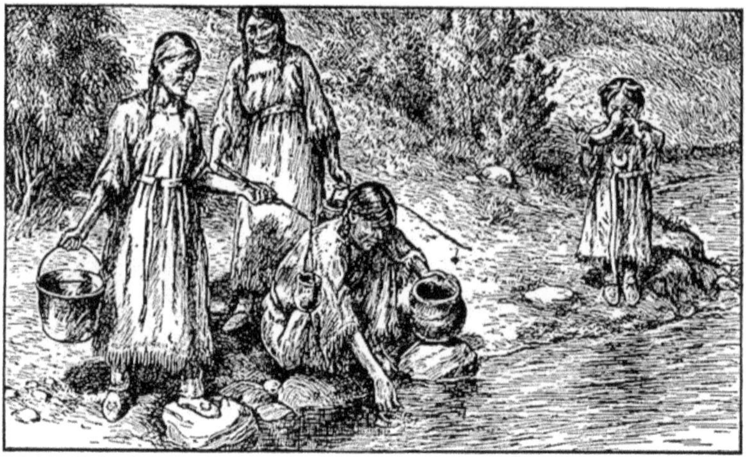

TENTH CHAPTER

LEARNING TO WORK

My mothers began to teach me household tasks when I was about twelve years old. "You are getting to be a big girl," they said. "Soon you will be a woman, and marry. Unless you learn to work, how will you feed your family?"

One of the things given me to do was fetching water from the river. No spring was near our village; and, anyhow, our prairie springs are often bitter with alkali. But the Missouri river, fed by melting snows of the Montana mountains, gave us plenty of fresh water. Missouri river water is muddy; but it soon settles, and is cool and sweet to drink. We Indians love our big river, and we are glad to drink of its waters, as drank our fathers.

A steep path led down the bank to the watering place. Down this path, the village girls made their way every morning to get water for drinking and cooking. They went in little groups or in pairs. Two girls, cousins or chums, sometimes swung a freshly filled pail from a pole on their shoulders.

But there were few pails of metal in my tribe, when I was a little girl. I used to fetch water in a clay pot, sometimes in a buffalo-paunch lining skewered on a stick; but my commonest bucket was of a buffalo heart skin. When my father killed a buffalo, he took out the heart skin, and filled it with grass until it dried. This he gave to Red Blossom, who sewed a little stick on each side of the mouth; and bound a short stick and sinews between them for handle. Such a bucket held about three pints. It was a frail looking vessel, but lasted a long time.

We girls liked to go to the watering place; for, while we were filling our buckets, we could gossip with our friends. For older girls and young men it was a place for courtship. A youth, with painted face and trailing hair switch, would loiter near the path, and smile slyly at his sweetheart as she passed. She did not always smile back. Sometimes for long weeks, she held her eyes away, not even glancing at his moccasins. It was a shy smile that she gave him, at last. Nor did she talk with her love-boy—as we called him—when others were about. We should have thought that silly. But he might wait for her at sunset, by her father's lodge, and talk with her in the twilight.

But I had other tasks besides fetching water. I learned to cook, sweep, and sew with awl and sinew. Red Blossom taught me to embroider with quills of gull and porcupine, dyed in colors. Sometimes I helped at harder work; gathered drift wood at the river, dressed or scraped hides, and even helped in our cornfield.

I liked to go with my mothers to the cornfields in planting time, when the spring sun was shining and the birds singing in the tree tops. How good it seemed to be out under the open sky, after the long months in our winter camp! A cottonwood tree stood at a turn of the road to our field. Every season a pair of magpies built their nest in it. They were saucy birds and scolded us roundly when we passed. How I used to laugh at their wicked scoldings!

I am afraid I did not help my mothers much. Like any young girl, I liked better to watch the birds than to work. Sometimes I chased away the crows. Our corn indeed had many enemies, and we had to watch that they did not get our crop. Magpies and crows destroyed much of the young corn. Crows were fond of pulling up the plants when they were a half inch or an inch high. Spotted gophers dug up the roots of the young corn, to nibble the soft seed.

When our field was all planted, Red Blossom used to go back and replant any hills that the birds had destroyed. Where she found a plant missing, she dug a little hole with her hand and dropped in a seed, or I dropped it in for her.

It was hard work, stooping to plant in the hot sun, and Red Blossom never liked having to go over the field a second time. "Those bad crows," she would groan, "they make us much trouble."

My grandmother Turtle made scarecrows to frighten away the birds. In the middle of the field she drove two sticks for legs, and bound two other sticks to them for arms; on the top, she fastened a ball of cast-away skins for a head. She belted an old robe about the figure to make it look like a man. Such a scarecrow looked wicked! Indeed I was almost afraid of it myself. But the bad crows, seeing the scarecrow never moved from its place, soon lost their fear, and came back.

In the months of midsummer, the crows did not give us much trouble; but, as the moon of Cherries drew near, they became worse than ever. The corn had now begun to ear, and crows and blackbirds came in flocks to peck open the green ears for the soft kernels. Many families now built stages in their fields, where the girls and young women of the household came to sit and sing as they watched that crows and other thieves did not steal the ripening grain.

We cared for our corn in those days, as we would care for a child; for we Indian people loved our fields as mothers love their children. We thought that the corn plants had souls, as children have souls, and that the growing corn liked to hear us sing, as children like to hear their mothers sing to them. Nor did we want the birds to come and steal our corn, after the hard work of planting and hoeing. Horses, too, might break into the field, or boys might steal the green ears and go off and roast them.

A watchers' stage was not hard to build. Four posts, forked at the tops, upheld beams, on which was laid a floor of puncheons, or split small logs, at the height of the full grown corn. The floor was about four feet long by three wide, roomy enough for two girls to sit together comfortably. Often a soft robe was spread on the floor. A ladder made of the trunk of a tree rested against the stage. The ladder had three steps.

A tree was often left standing in the field, to shade the watchers' stage. If the tree was small and more shade was wanted, a robe was stretched over three poles leaned against the stage. These poles could be shifted with the sun.

Girls began to go on the watchers' stage when about ten or twelve years of age, and many kept up the custom after they were grown up and married. Older women, working in the field and stopping to rest, often went on the stage and sang.

There was a watchers' stage in my mothers' field, where my sister, Cold Medicine, and I sat and sang; and in the two weeks of the ripening season we were singing most of the time. We looked upon watching our field as a kind of lark. We liked to sing, and now and then between songs we stood up to see if horses had broken into the field or if any boys were about. Boys of nine or ten years of age were quite troublesome. They liked to steal the green ears to roast by a fire in the woods.

I think Cold Medicine and I were rather glad to catch a boy stealing our corn, especially if he was a clan cousin, for then we could call him all the bad names we wished. "You bad, bad boy," we would cry. "You thief,—stealing from your own relatives! *Nah, nah,*—go away." This was enough; no boy stayed after such a scolding.

Most of the songs we sang were love-boy songs, as we called them; but not all were. One that we younger girls were fond of singing—girls, that is, of about twelve years of age—was like this:

You bad boys, you are all alike!

Your bow is like a bent basket hoop;

Your arrows are fit only to shoot into the air;

You poor boys, you must run on the prairie barefoot, because you have no moccasins!

This song we sang to tease the boys who came to hunt birds in the near-by woods. Small boys went bird hunting nearly every day. The birds that a boy snared or shot he gave to his grandparents to roast in the lodge fire; for, with their well-worn teeth, old people could no longer chew our hard, dried buffalo meat.

Here is another song; but, that you may understand it, I will explain to you what *eekupa*[20] means. A girl loved by another girl as her own sister was called her *eekupa*. I think your word "chum," as you explain it, has nearly the same meaning. This is the song:

"My *eekupa*, what do you wish to see?" you said to me.

What I wish to see is the corn silk peeping out of the growing ear;

But what *you* wish to see is that naughty young man coming!

[20] ēē´ kụ pä

Here is a song that older girls sang to tease young men of the Dog Society who happened to be going by:

You young man of the Dog Society, you said to me,

"When I go east with a war party, you will hear news of me how brave I am!"

I have heard news of you;

When the fight was on, you ran and hid;

And you still think you are a brave young man!

Behold, you have joined the Dog Society;

But I call you just plain *dog*!

Songs that we sang on the watchers' stage we called *meedaheeka*,[21] or gardeners' songs. I have said that many of them were love-boy songs, and were intended to tease. We called a girl's sweetheart her love-boy. All girls, we know, like to tease their sweethearts.

[21] mēē dä´ hēē kä

At one side of our field Turtle had made a booth, diamond willows thrust in the ground in a circle, with leafy tops bent over and tied together. In this booth, my sister and I, with our mothers and old Turtle, cooked our meals. We started a fire in the booth as soon as we got to the field, and ate our breakfast often at sunrise. Our food we had brought with us, usually buffalo meat, fresh or dried. Fresh meat we laid on the coals to broil. Dried meat we thrust on a stick and held over the fire to toast.

Sometimes we brought a clay cooking pot, and boiled squashes. We were fond of squashes and ate many of them. We sometimes boiled green corn and beans. My sister and I shelled the corn from the cob. We shelled the beans or boiled them in the pod. My grandmother poured the mess in a wooden bowl, and we ate with spoons which she made from squash stems. She would split a stem with her knife and put in a little stick to hold the split open.

I do not think anything can taste sweeter than a mess of fresh corn and beans, in the cool morning air, when the birds are twittering and the sun is just peeping over the tree tops.

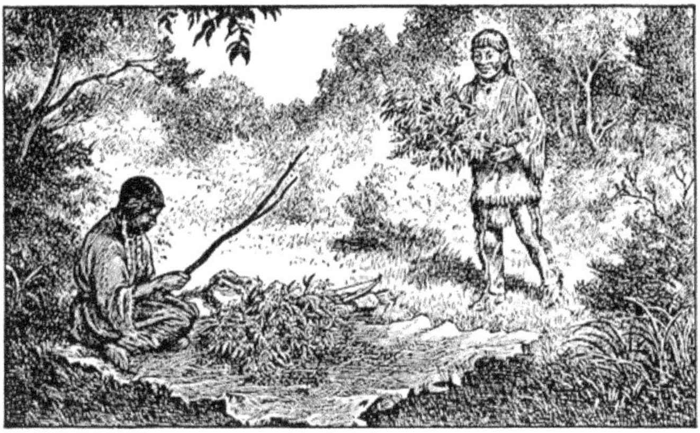

ELEVENTH CHAPTER

PICKING JUNE BERRIES

June berry time had come. I was now fourteen years, old and had begun to think myself almost a young woman. Some of the young men even smiled at me as I came up from the watering place. I never smiled back, for I thought: "My father is a chief, and I belong to one of the best families in my tribe. I will be careful whom I choose to be my friends."

A little north of my father's, stood the earth lodge of Bear Man's family. Bear Man was an eagle hunter. He had magic snares of sacred hemp plant which he tossed into the air as he prayed to the eagle spirits. After doing so he was sure to catch many young golden eagles at his eagle pit. We thought him a great medicine man.

Bear Man had a son named Sacred-Red-Eagle-Wing, a straight-limbed, rather good-looking lad, a year older than myself. Bear Man's father died, and Bear Man cut off his long hair in mourning. Sacred-Red-Eagle-Wing made a switch of his father's hair, tastefully spotting it with little lumps of spruce gum mixed with red ochre. He looked quite manly, I thought, wearing this switch, in spite of his fifteen years.

My father's earth lodge and Bear Man's both faced eastward, with the lodge of Blue Paint's family standing between; but, as I stood at my father's lodge entrance, I could see the flat top of Bear Man's lodge over Blue Paint's roof. Sacred-Red-Eagle-Wing had joined the Stone Hammer Society a short while before, and had begun to paint his face like a young man. He would get up on his father's roof, painted, and decked out in hair switch, best leggings, and moccasins, and sing his society's songs. He had a fine voice, I thought; and when I went out with my buck-brush broom to sweep the ground about our lodge entrance, Sacred-Red-Eagle-Wing would sing harder than ever. I thought perhaps he did this so that I would hear him. I was too well-bred to look up at him, but I did not always hurry to finish my sweeping.

There had been plenty of rain, and the June berry trees were now loaded with ripe fruit. We Indians set great store by these berries, and almost every family dried one or more sackfuls for winter. June berries are sweet, and, as we had no sugar, we were fond of them.

We were sitting one evening at our supper. Red Blossom had gone into the woods earlier in the day and fetched home some ripe June berries which we were eating. Perhaps that is why we ended our meal with our kettle half-full of boiled meat. "We will save this meat until morning," Red Blossom said. "We must breakfast early, for Strikes-Many Woman and I are going with a party to pick June berries. Our daughter may go with us, if she will."

I was quite happy when I heard this. I had seen my two mothers getting ready their berry sacks; and, looking over to the bench where they lay, I now saw that a small sack had been laid out for me.

Red Blossom dipped her fingers into the kettle for a lump of fat and continued: "The mother of that young man, Sacred-Red-Eagle-Wing, said to me to-day, 'If your daughter goes berrying to-morrow, my son wishes to go with her. He will take his bow and keep off enemies.'"

I did not blush, for we Indian girls had dark skins and painted our cheeks; but I felt my heart jump. I looked down at the floor, then got up and went about my work, humming a song as I did so; for I thought, "I am going berrying in the morning." I felt quite grown-up to know that a young man wanted to go berrying with me.

We were off the next morning before the sun was up. I walked with my mothers and the other women. The men went a little ahead, armed, some with guns, others with bows. Sacred-Red-Eagle-Wing walked behind the men. On his back I saw a handsome otter-skin quiver, full of arrows. I felt safer to see those arrows. Enemies might be lurking anywhere in the woods, ready to capture us or take our scalps. We Indian women dared not go far into the woods without men to protect us.

At the woods the men joined us, and our party broke up into little groups, the older men helping their wives, and the younger men their sweethearts. I made my way to a clump of June berry trees bent nearly to the ground with fruit. I did not look to see if Sacred-Red-Eagle-Wing was following me. I thought, "If he wants to help me, he may; but I shall not ask him." I spread a skin under the branches, and I was looking for a stout stick when I saw my boy friend breaking off the laden branches and piling them on the skin, ready to be beaten.

I sat on the ground and with my stick beat off the berries. Sacred-Red-Eagle-Wing fetched me fresh branches, and in an hour or two I had enough berries to fill my sack. Sacred-Red-Eagle-Wing's arrows lay at my feet. Once, when a near-by bush stirred, my boy friend leaped for his bow and laid an arrow on the string; but it was the wind, I guess.

All the time that we worked together Sacred-Red-Eagle-Wing and I spoke not a word. Older couples, I knew, talked together, when they thought of marrying; but I was a young girl yet and did not want to be bothered with a husband.

When my sack was filled, I tied it shut and slung it on my back by my packing strap. Sacred-Red-Eagle-Wing laid some sweet smelling leaves under the sack that the juices from the ripe berries might not ooze through and stain my dress.

I am sorry to say that I am not sure I even thanked Sacred-Red-Eagle-Wing for all he did to help me.

I walked back to the village with the women as I had come. Ahead of us walked a young woman named Pink Blossom, with her chin in the air as if she were angry. The older women, coming after her, were laughing and slyly jesting with one another. I asked my mothers what it was all about.

It seems there was an old man in our party named Old Bear, whose wife had died. He wanted to marry again and smiled at Pink Blossom whenever she passed him; but she did not like Old Bear, and she turned her eyes away whenever he came near.

When she came to the June berry woods, Pink Blossom set her sack under a tree, while she picked berries. Old Bear saw the sack. He folded his robe under his arm into a kind of pocket, picked it full of berries, and emptied them into Pink Blossom's sack.

This vexed Pink Blossom. She went to her sack and poured Old Bear's berries out on the ground. "I do not want that old man to smile at me," she told the other women.

It was because the women were laughing at her and Old Bear, that Pink Blossom walked ahead with her chin in the air. The others were having a good deal of fun with one another at her expense.

"I think Pink Blossom did wrong to waste the berries," said one, a clan cousin. "If she did not want them herself, she should have given them back to Old Bear, for him to eat."

"Old Bear's is a sad case," said Elk Woman. "But I knew a man in a worse case."

"Tell us of it," said Red Blossom.

"Years ago," said Elk Woman, "I went berrying with some others on the other side of the Missouri. In the party was a young man named Weasel Arm. He was a good singer, and he liked to sing so that his sweetheart could hear his voice. His sweetheart was also in the party. Weasel Arm helped her fill her sack; and when she went back with the other women and they were waiting for some that had not yet come in, Weasel Arm lay down on the grass a little way off and sang, beating time on the stock of his gun.

"As he lay there he heard some one riding toward him, but thought it was one of his party. It was a Sioux; and right in the midst of the song—*poh!*—the Sioux fired, wounding Weasel Arm in the hip. Luckily the wound was slight, and Weasel Arm sprang for the near-by woods. The Sioux dared not follow him, for he saw that Weasel Arm had a gun."

"I do not think Weasel Arm's case as sad as Old Bear's," said one of the women. "Weasel Arm was wounded in his body, but Old Bear is wounded in his heart."

Elk Woman laughed. "Have no fear for Old Bear," she said. "He is an old man and has had more than one sweetheart. His heart will soon heal."

"But I am sorry for the spilled berries," she continued. "Pink Blossom should not waste good berries, even if Old Bear does look like an old man."

All laughed at this but Pink Blossom.

"I knew a young woman who once wasted good rose berries, just as Pink Blossom wasted the June berries," said Old-Owl Woman.

"Tell us the story," said one of my mothers.

"When I was a girl," said Old-Owl Woman, "Ear-Eat, a Crow Indian, married Yellow Blossom, a Hidatsa girl. They went to live with the Crows, but after a year they came back to visit our tribe at Five Villages.

"It was in the fall, when the rose berries are ripe. Now the Crow Indians like to eat rose berries, and gather them to dry for winter as we dry squashes. We Hidatsas eat rose berries sometimes, but we never dry them for winter. We think they are food for wild men.

"Ear-Eat was riding in the woods near our villages, when he found a thicket of rose bushes bending over with their load of ripe berries. '*Ey*,' he cried, 'how many berries are here! I never saw it thus in our Crow country.' And he got off his horse and began to pick the berries.

"He had no basket to put them in, so he drew off his leggings, tied the bottoms shut with his moccasin strings, and, when he had filled the leggings with berries, he slung them over his horse's back like a pair of saddle bags.

"He rode home happy, for he thought, 'My wife will be glad to see so many berries.'

"When Yellow Blossom saw her husband riding home without his leggings, and with the tops of his moccasins loose and flapping, she could hardly believe her eyes. As she stood staring, Ear-Eat got off his horse and handed her his bulging leggings. 'Here, wife,' he cried, 'look at these fine berries. Now we shall have something good to eat.'

"The village women, hearing what Ear-Eat said, crowded close to look. When they saw that his leggings were filled with rose berries, they cried out with laughter.

"Yellow Blossom was angry. 'You are crazy,' she cried to her husband. 'We Hidatsas raise corn, beans, sunflower seed, and good squashes to eat. We are not starving, that we must eat rose berries.'

"'The Crow Indians eat rose berries,' said Ear-Eat. 'My mother used to dry them for winter food.'

"His words but vexed Yellow Blossom more.

"'I am a Hidatsa woman, not a Crow,' she cried. 'We Hidatsas are not wild people. We live in earth lodges and eat foods from our gardens. When we go berrying we put our berries into clean baskets, not into our leggings.' And she turned the leggings up and poured the rose berries out on the ground."

We all laughed at Old-Owl Woman's story.

"We had other use for rose berries when I was a girl," said Red Blossom. "If a young man went at evening to talk with his sweetheart, he put a ripe rose berry in his mouth to make his breath sweet."

"I wonder if Old Bear put a rose berry in his mouth," said Old-Owl Woman.

"I think he put two rose berries in his mouth," said Red Blossom, smiling.

All laughed again but Pink Blossom; she walked on, saying nothing.

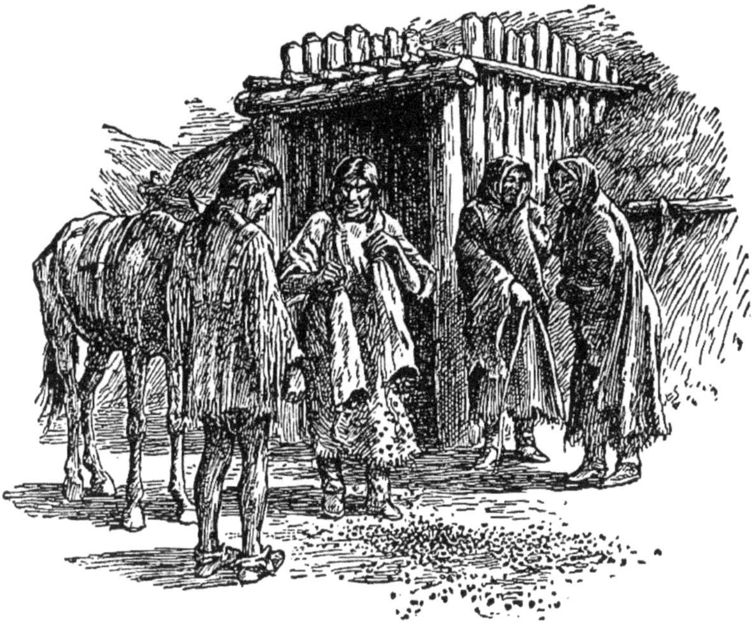

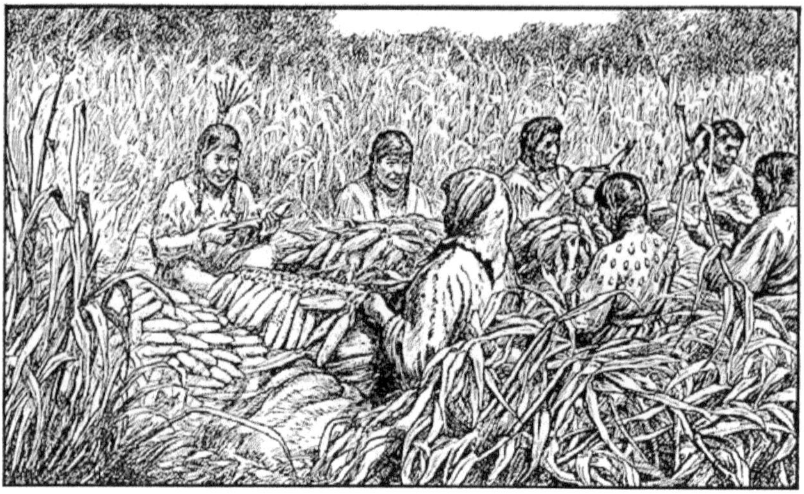

TWELFTH CHAPTER

THE CORN HUSKING

After the June berry season came choke-cherries. We did not gather so big a store of these, but they were harder to prepare for drying. I can yet see old Turtle, with her gnarled, wrinkled fingers, plying the crushing stones. She dropped three or four cherries on a round stone and crushed them with a smaller stone held in her palm. The pulp she squeezed through her palms into lumps, which she dried in the sun.

And then came the corn harvest, busiest and happiest time of all the year. It was hard work gathering and husking the corn, but what fun we had! For days we girls thought of nothing but the fine dresses we should wear at the husking.

While the ears were ripening my sister and I went every morning to sit on our watch stage and sing to the corn. One evening we brought home with us a basketful of the green ears and were husking them by the fire. My father gathered up the husks and took them out of the lodge. I wondered why he did so.

"I fed the husks, daughter, to my pack horses," he said, when he came back. "To-morrow I go hunting to get meat for the husking." He had brought his hunting pony into the lodge, but he had penned his pack horses for the night under the corn stage.

My two mothers, I knew, were planning a big feast. "We have much corn to husk," they said, "and we must have plenty of food, for we do not want our huskers to go away hungry."

Small Ankle left us before daybreak. He returned the fourth day after, about noon, with two deer loaded on his pack horses. "One is a black-tail," he told us when he came in the lodge, "a buck that I killed yesterday in some bad lands by the Little Missouri. He was hiding in a clump of trees. As I rode near, he winded me and ran out into the open. I checked my pony, and the buck stopped to look around. I fired, and he fell; but, when I got off my horse, the buck rose and tried to push me with his horns. I killed him with my knife." A wounded black-tail often tried to fight off the hunters: a white-tail hardly ever did so.

The next morning we women rose early, and with our baskets hastened to the cornfield. All day we plucked the ripe ears, bearing them in our baskets to the center of the field, where we laid them in a long pile. That night my father and Red Blossom slept on the watchers' stage, to see that no horse broke in and trampled our corn pile. There was not much danger of this.

Around the field ran a kind of fence, of willows, enough to keep out the ponies.

The rest of us returned to the lodge to make ready for the feast the next day. Turtle fetched out three great bundles of dried buffalo meat and piled them on the puncheon bench with the freshly killed deer meat. Our three kettles were scoured and set by, ready to be taken to the field.

At nightfall Bear's Tail went around the village to lodges of our relatives and friends, and invited the young men to come to our husking.

I was too excited that night to sleep much. Early in the morning my sister and I rose and went to the river for a dip in its cold waters. After a hasty breakfast I put on my best dress, of deer skin, with hoofs hanging like bangles at the edge of the skirt and three rows of costly elk teeth across the front. Cold Medicine helped me paint my face, and was careful to rub a little red ochre in the part of my hair.

The sun was just coming over the prairie when we started for the field. We had loaded our kettles and meat on two pack horses, and old Turtle led the way. My father and Red Blossom had risen early and eaten breakfast, and now had a brisk fire going. We put our kettles on, after filling them with water. In one we put dried, in another fresh, meat; the third kettle we filled with green corn, late planted for this purpose. The meat and corn were for our feast.

The sun was three hours high when the huskers came. They were about thirty in all, young men, except three or four crippled old warriors who wanted to feast. These were too old to work much, but my father made them welcome.

The huskers came into the field yelling and singing. We had, indeed, heard their yells long before we saw them. I think young men all sing and yell, just because they are young.

My sister and I were already seated at one side of the corn pile, and the other women joined us. The young men sat down on the opposite side, and the husking began.

I saw that Sacred-Red-Eagle-Wing sat just opposite me. Next to him was a young man named Red Hand, with grass plumes in his hair. These meant that he had been in a war party and had been sent out to spy on the enemy. I saw Red Hand looking at me, and I was glad that I was wearing my elk teeth dress. "He is a young man," I thought, "not a boy, like Sacred-Red-Eagle-Wing."

The huskers worked rapidly, stripping off the dry husks with their hands. The big fine ears they braided in strings, to save for seed. Smaller ears they tossed into a pile. Big as our corn pile was, it was husked in about four hours.

My mothers then served the feast. The huskers were hearty eaters; for, like all young men, they had good appetites; but we had a big feast of meat, and even they could not eat all. It was not polite to leave any of the food, and some had brought sharp sticks on which they skewered the meat they could not eat, to take home with them.

The feast over, the huskers went to another field, singing and yelling as they went.

We women had now to busy ourselves carrying in our corn.

We loaded our two pack horses with strings of braided ears, ten strings to a pony. The smaller ears we bore to the village in our baskets, to dry on our corn stage before threshing.

In midafternoon there were a few strings of corn still left, and I was laying them by for the next trip when I heard steps. I looked up and saw Red Hand coming, leading his pony.

Red Hand did not speak, but he laid my strings of corn on his pony and started for the village. "He wants to help me take home my corn," I thought. A young man did thus for the girl he admired. "Red Hand is brave, and he owns a pony," I said to myself; and I forgot all about Sacred-Red-Eagle-Wing.

My father returned with the pack horses just as Red Hand was starting off; and I was stooping to fill my basket, when suddenly there came a sound, *poh-poh-poh*, as of guns; then yells, and a woman screamed. Small Ankle sprang for his war pony, which he had left hobbled near the husking pile.

Our corn fields lay in a strip of flat land skirted by low foot hills; and now I saw, coming over the hills, a party of Sioux, thirty or more, mounted, and painted for war. At the edge of the hills they checked their ponies, and those who had guns began firing down into our gardens. Many of the Sioux were armed with bows and arrows.

On all sides arose outcries. My brave father dashed by with his ringing war whoop, *ui, ui, ui*;[22] and after him Red Hand, lashing his pony and yelling like mad. Red Hand had thrown away my strings of corn, but I was not thinking of my corn just then.

[22] ṳ ï (pronounced like ōō ēē, but quickly and sharply)

Women and children began streaming past our field to the village. Brave young men rode between them and our enemies, lest the Sioux dash down and cut off some straggler. Two lads, on swift ponies, galloped ahead to rouse the villagers.

Meanwhile my father and others were fighting off the Sioux from the shelter of some clumps of small trees that dotted the flat: Our enemies did not fight standing, but galloped and pranced their horses about on the hillside to spoil our aim.

Suddenly a Sioux warrior, in trailing eagle-feather bonnet, and mounted on a beautiful spotted pony, dashed down the hillside toward us, waving his bow over his head; and from our side I saw Red Hand, gun in hand, riding to meet him.

As they drew near one another the Sioux swerved, and an arrow, like a little snake, came curving through the air. Red Hand's pony stumbled and fell, the shaft in its throat; but Red Hand, leaping to the ground, raised his gun and fired. I saw the Sioux drop his bow and ride back clinging desperately to his pony's mane. Red Hand put his hand to his mouth and I heard his *yi-yi-yi-yi-yah*,[23] the yell that a warrior made when he had wounded an enemy.

[23] yĭ yĭ yĭ yĭ yäh´

On the side toward our village other cries now arose, for the warriors were coming to our help. The Sioux fled. Our men pursued them, and at nightfall came back with one scalp.

All that night we danced the scalp dance. A big fire was built. Men and women painted their faces black and sang glad songs. Old women cried *a-la-la-la-la!*[24] Young men danced, yelled and boasted of their deeds. All said that Red Hand was a brave young man and would become a great warrior.

[24] ä lä lä lä lä´

The next day I was coming from the watering place with my kettle. Just ahead of me walked Waving Corn, a handsome girl two years older than I. Red Hand passed by; shyly I looked up, thinking to see him smile at me.

He was smiling at Waving Corn.

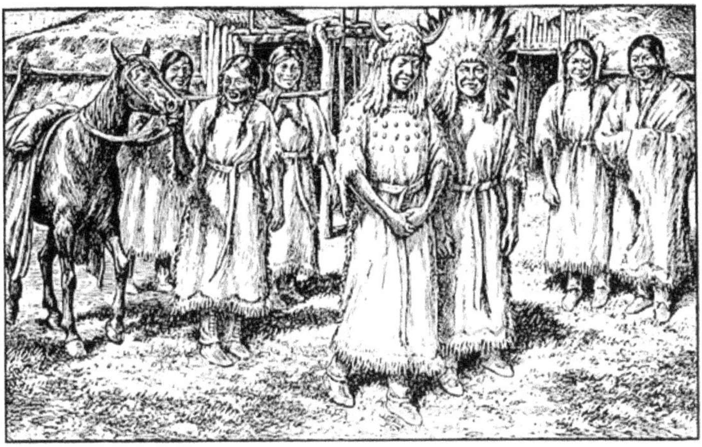

THIRTEENTH CHAPTER

MARRIAGE

And so I grew up, a happy, contented Indian girl, obedient to my mothers, but loving them dearly. I learned to cook, dress skins, embroider, sew with awl and sinew, and cut and make moccasins, clothing and tent covers. There was always plenty of work to do, but I had time to rest, and to go to see my friends; and I was not given tasks beyond my strength. My father did the heavy lifting, if posts or beams were to be raised. "You are young, daughter," he would say. "Take care you do not overstrain!" He was a kind man, and helped my mothers and me whenever we had hard work to do.

For my industry in dressing skins, my clan aunt, Sage, gave me a woman's belt. It was as broad as my three fingers, and covered with blue beads. One end was made long, to hang down before me. Only a very industrious girl was given such a belt. She could not buy or make one. No relative could give her the belt; for a clan aunt, remember, was not a blood relative. To wear a woman's belt was an honor. I was as proud of mine as a war leader of his first scalp.

I won other honors by my industry. For embroidering a robe for my father with porcupine quills I was given a brass ring, bought of the traders; and for embroidering a tent cover with gull quills dyed yellow and blue I was given a bracelet. There were few girls in the village who owned belt, ring and bracelet.

In these years of my girlhood my mothers were watchful of all that I did. We had big dances in the village, when men and women sang, drums beat loud, and young men, painted and feathered, danced and yelled to show their brave deeds. I did not go to these dances often, and, when I did, my mothers went with me. Ours was one of the better families of the tribe, and my mothers were very careful of me.

I was eighteen years old the Bent-Enemy-Killed winter; for we Hidatsas reckoned by winters, naming each for something that happened in it. An old man named Hanging Stone then lived in the village. He had a stepson named Magpie, a handsome young man and a good hunter.

One morning Hanging Stone came into our lodge. It was a little while after our morning meal, and I was putting away the wooden bowls that we used for dishes. The hollow buffalo hoofs hung on the door for bells, I remember, rattled clitter, clitter, clitter, as he raised and let fall the door. My father was sitting by the fire.

Hanging Stone walked up to my father, and laid his right hand on my father's head. "I want you to believe what I say," he cried. "I want my boy to live in your good family. I am poor, you are rich; but I want you to favor us and do as I ask."

He went over to my mothers and did likewise, speaking the same words to both. He then strode out of the lodge.

Neither my father nor my mothers said anything, and I did not know at first what it all meant. My father sat for a while, looking at the fire. At last he spoke, "My daughter is too young to marry. When she is older I may be willing."

Toward evening Hanging Stone and his relatives brought four horses and three flint-lock guns to our lodge. He tied the four horses to the drying stage outside. They had good bridles, with chains hanging to the bits. On the back of each horse was a blanket and some yards of calico, very expensive in those days.

Hanging Stone came into the lodge. "I have brought you four horses and three guns," he said to my father.

"I must refuse them," answered Small Ankle. "My daughter is too young to marry."

Hanging Stone went away, but he did not take his horses with him. My father sent them back by some young men.

The evening of the second day after, Hanging Stone came again to our lodge. As before, he brought the three guns and gifts of cloth, and four horses; but two of these were hunting horses. A hunting horse was one fleet enough to overtake a buffalo, a thing that few of our little Indian ponies could do. Such horses were costly and hard to get. A family that had good hunting horses had always plenty of meat.

After Hanging Stone left, my father said to his wives, "What do you think about it?"

"We would rather not say anything," they answered. "Do as you think best."

"I know this Magpie," said my father. "He is a kind young man. I have refused his gifts once, but I see his heart is set on having our daughter. I think I shall agree to it."

Turning to me he spoke: "My daughter, I have tried to raise you right. I have hunted and worked hard to give you food to eat. Now I want you to take my advice. Take this man for your husband. Try always to love him. Do not think in your heart, 'I am a handsome young woman, but this man, my husband, is older and not handsome.' Never taunt your husband. Try not to do anything that will make him angry."

I did not answer *yes* or *no* to this; for I thought, "If my father wishes me to do this, why that is the best thing for me to do." I had been taught to be obedient to my father. I do not think white children are taught so, as we Indian children were taught.

For nigh a week my father and my two mothers were busy getting ready the feast foods for the wedding. On the morning of the sixth day, my father took from his bag a fine weasel-skin cap and an eagle-feather war bonnet. The first he put on my head; the second he handed to my sister, Cold Medicine. "Take these to Hanging Stone's lodge," he said.

We were now ready to march. I led, my sister walking with me. Behind us came some of our relatives, leading three horses; and, after them, five great kettles of feast foods, on poles borne on the shoulders of women relatives. The kettles held boiled dried green corn and ripe corn pounded to meal and boiled with beans; and they were steaming hot.

There was a covered entrance to Hanging Stone's lodge. The light was rather dim inside, and I did not see a dog lying there until he sprang up, barking *wu-wu!* and dashed past me. I sprang back, startled. Cold Medicine tittered. "Do not be foolish," called one of our women relatives. Cold Medicine stopped her tittering, but I think we were rather glad of the dog. My sister and I had never marched in a wedding before, and we were both a little scared.

I lifted the skin door—it was an old-fashioned one swinging on thongs from the beam overhead—and entered the lodge. Hanging Stone sat on his couch against the puncheon fire screen. I went to him and put the weasel-skin cap on his head. The young man who was to be my husband was sitting on his couch, a frame of poles covered with a tent skin. Cold Medicine and I went over and shyly sat on the floor near-by.

The kettles of feast foods had been set down near the fireplace, and the three horses tied to the corn stage without. Hanging Stone had fetched my father four horses. We reckoned the weasel cap and the war bonnet as worth each a horse; and, with these and our three horses, my father felt he was going his friend one horse better. It was a point of honor in an Indian family for the bride's father to make a more valuable return gift than that brought him by the bridegroom and his friends.

Plate II.—"I put the weasel-skin cap on his head."

As we two girls sat on the floor, with ankles to the right, as Indian women always sit, Magpie's mother filled a wooden bowl with dried buffalo meat pounded fine and mixed with marrow fat, and set it for my sister and me to eat. We ate as much as we could. What was left, my sister put in a fold of her robe, and we arose and went home. It would have been impolite to leave behind any of the food given us to eat.

Later in the day Magpie's relatives and friends came to feast on the foods we had taken to Hanging Stone's lodge. Each guest brought a gift, something useful to a new-wed bride—beaded work, fawn-skin work bag, girl's leggings, belt, blanket, woman's robe, calico for a dress, and the like. In the evening two women of Magpie's family brought these gifts to my father's lodge, packing them each in a blanket on her back. They piled the gifts on the floor beside Red Blossom, the elder of my two mothers.

Red Blossom spent the next few days helping me build and decorate the couch that was to mark off the part of our lodge set apart for my husband and me. We even made and placed before the couch a fine, roomy lazy-back, or willow chair.

All being now ready, Red Blossom said to me: "Go and call your husband. Go and sit beside him and say, 'I want you to come to my father's lodge.' Do not feel shy. Go boldly and have no fear."

So with my sister I slowly walked to Hanging Stone's lodge. There were several besides the family within, for they were expecting me; but no one said anything as we entered.

Magpie was sitting on his couch, for this in the daytime was used as white men use a lounge or a big chair. My sister and I went over and sat beside him. Magpie smiled and said, "What have you come for?"

"I have come to call you," I answered.

"*Sukkeets*—good!" he said.

Cold Medicine and I arose and returned to my father's lodge. Magpie followed us a few minutes later; for young men did not walk through the village with their sweethearts in the daytime. We should have thought that foolish.

And so I was wed.

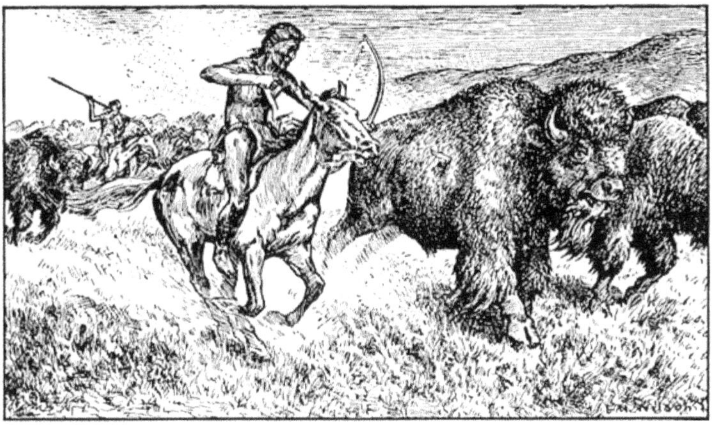

FOURTEENTH CHAPTER

A BUFFALO HUNT

My young husband and I lived together but a few years. He died of lung sickness; and, after I had mourned a year, I married Son-of-a-Star, a Mandan. My family wished me to marry again; for, while an Indian woman could raise corn for herself and family, she could not hunt to get meat and skins.

Son-of-a-Star was a kind man, and my father liked him. "He is brave, daughter," Small Ankle said. "He wears two eagle feathers, for he has twice struck an enemy, and he has danced the death dance. Three times he has shot an arrow through a buffalo." It was not easy to shoot an arrow through a buffalo and few of my tribe had done so.

Spring had come, and in the moon of Breaking Ice we returned to Like-a-Fishhook village. Our hunters had not killed many deer the winter before, and our stores of corn were getting low. As ours was a large family, Son-of-a-Star thought he would join a hunting party that was going up the river for buffaloes. "Even if we do not find much game," he said, "we shall kill enough for ourselves. We younger men should not be eating the corn and beans that old men and children need."

Small Ankle thought the plan a good one. I was glad also, for I was to be one of the party. Corn planting time would not come for a month yet; and, after the weeks in our narrow winter quarters, I longed to be out again in the fresh air.

There were ten in the party besides Son-of-a-Star and myself: Crow-Flies-High, Bad Brave, High Backbone, Long Bear, and Scar, and their wives. Scar was a Teton Sioux who had come to visit us.

My tribe now owned many horses, and fewer dogs were used than when I was a little girl. A party of buffalo hunters usually took both hunting and pack horses; but our village herd was weak and poor in flesh after the scant winter's feeding, and we thought it better to take only dogs. There was yet little pasture, and the ground was wet and spongy from the spring thaws. Only a strong, well-fed pony could go all day on wet ground.

I took three of our family dogs. On the travois of two I loaded robes for bedding, the halves of an old tent cover, moccasins for myself and husband, an ax, a copper kettle and a flesher for dressing hides. My third dog dragged a bull boat, bound mouth down to the travois poles. We planned to return by way of the river, in boats.

We were clad warmly, for the weather was chill. All had robes. I wore a dress of two deer skins sewed edge to edge; the hind legs, thus sewed, made the sleeves for my arms.

I had made my husband a fine skin shirt, embroidered with beads. Over it he drew his robe, fur side in. He spread his feet apart, drew the robe high enough to cover his head, and folded it, tail end first, over his right side; then the head end over his left, and belted the robe in place. He spread his feet apart when belting, to give the robe a loose skirt for walking in.

We all wore winter moccasins, fur lined, with high tops. The men carried guns. Buffalo hunters no longer used bows except from horseback.

We started off gaily, in a long line. Each woman was followed by her dogs. Two women, having no dogs, packed their camp stuff on their backs.

We made our first camp late in the afternoon, at a place called Timber-Faces-across-River. There was a spring here, of good water. Crow-Flies-High and Bad Brave went hunting, while we women pitched our tent. We cut forked poles and stacked them with tops together like a tepee. We covered this frame with skins, laced together at the edges with thongs. A rawhide lariat was drawn around the outside of the cover; and small logs, laid about the edges, held the tent to the ground. We could not use tent pins, for the ground was frozen. We raised an old saddle skin on the windward side of the smoke hole, staying it with a forked pole, thrust through a hole in the edge. We were some time building, as the tent had to be large enough for twelve persons.

We finished just at dusk; and we were starting a fire inside, when the two hunters came in. Each packed on his back the side and ham of an elk they had killed. Bad Brave had laid a pad of dry grass across his shoulders that the meat juice might not stain his robe.

It was getting dark, and, while we women gathered dry grass for our beds, the two hunters roasted one of the sides of meat. They skewered it on a stick and swung it from the drying pole. Standing on each side, the two men swung the meat slowly, forth and back, over the fire.

We were all hungry when we sat down to eat. The fresh roasted ribs of the elk were juicy and sweet, and with full stomachs we felt sleepy, for the day's march had been long. We gladly spread our robes and crept into our beds, first covering a coal with ashes for the morning fire.

Next morning we had struck our tent and loaded our dogs before the sun was well up. We took only the tent cover, leaving the poles. Three of our men went ahead to hunt. The rest followed more slowly, not to tire our dogs. Now and then we stopped to rest and eat from our lunch bags. These were of dried buffalo heart skins. Every woman in the party carried one of them tucked under her belt. We had been careful to fill our bags with cooked meat, from our breakfast.

My husband walked at my side if he talked with me. At other times he went a little ahead; for, if enemies or a grizzly attacked us, he would thus be in front, ready to fight, giving me time to escape.

Our trail led along the brow of the bluffs overlooking the Missouri. There was a path here, fairly well marked, made by hunting parties, and perhaps by buffaloes.

Our second camp was at a place called the Slides; for, here, big blocks of earth, softened by the spring rains, sometimes slide down the bank into the river. We found a spring a little way in from the river, with small trees that we could cut for tent poles.

Our tent was hardly pitched when Son-of-a-Star and Scar came in to say they had killed a stray buffalo not far away. They had packed part of the meat to camp on their shoulders, and Son-of-a-Star had cut out the buffalo's paunch and filled it with fresh blood. While the two hunters went back for the rest of the meat, I put on my copper kettle and made blood pudding. It was hot and ready to serve by the time they came back. I had stirred the pudding with a green chokecherry stick, giving it a pleasant, cherry flavor.

We were a jolly party as we sat around the evening fire. The hot pudding felt good in our stomachs, after the long march. My good dogs, Knife-Carrier, Took-a-Scalp, and Packs-a-Babe, I had fed with scraps of meat from the dead buffalo, and they were dozing outside, snuggled against the tent to keep warm. *Okeemeea*,[25] Crow-Flies-High's wife, fetched in some dry wood, which she put on the fire. A yellow blaze lit up the tent and a column of thin, blue smoke rose upward to the smoke hole.

[25] O kēē mēē´ ä

Crow-Flies-High filled his pipe and passed it among the men. Hidatsa women do not smoke.

In the morning, on the way up, we had forded a stream we call Rising Water creek. My leggings and moccasins were still wet; and, as I was wringing them out to dry over the fire, I said to High Backbone's wife Blossom: "That creek is dangerous. As I was fording it to-day, I slipped in the mud and nearly fell in; but I once got a good dinner out of that mud."

"How did you get a dinner out of mud?" asked Blossom.

"I will tell you," I answered. "I was a young girl then. My tribe had come up the river to hunt buffaloes and we had stopped at Rising Water Creek to make fires and eat our midday meal. It was summer and the creek was low, for there had been little rain. Some little girls went down for water. They came running back, much frightened. 'We saw something move in the mud of the creek,' they cried. 'It is alive!'

"We ran to the bank of the creek and, sure enough, something that looked as big as a man was struggling and floundering in a pool. The water was roiled and thick with mud.

"We could not think what it could be. Some thought it was an enemy trying to hide in the mud.

"A brave young man named Skunk threw off his leggings, drew his knife, and waded out to the thing. Suddenly he stooped, and in a moment started to land with the thing in his arms. It was a great fish, a sturgeon. It had a smooth back, like a catfish. We cut up the flesh and boiled it. It tasted sweet, like catfish flesh. I do not remember if we drank the broth, as we do when we boil catfish."

"I have seen those fish," said Bad Brave. "Sometimes when the Missouri falls after the spring floods, one of them will be left stranded on the sand; but I never knew one to be seen in Rising Water creek. I know that turtles are found there, the big kind that fight."

"I have heard that white men eat turtles," said Long Bear's wife. "I do not believe it."

"They do eat turtles," said High Backbone, "and they eat frogs. A white man told me. I asked him."

"*Ey!* And such unclean things; I could not eat them," cried Bird Woman.

"There are big turtles in our Dakota lakes," said Scar. "They are so big that they drag under the water buffaloes that come there to drink. I once heard a story of a magic turtle."

"Tell us the story," said Son-of-a-Star.

"A brave young Dakota led out a war party, of six men," began Scar. "They came into the Chippewa country and wandered about, seeking to strike an enemy. They found deserted camps, sometimes with ashes in the fire pit still warm; but they found no enemies.

"One day they came to a beautiful lake. On the shore, close to the water, was a grassy knoll, rising upward like the back of a great turtle.

"The leader of the party had now begun to lose heart. 'We have found no enemy,' he said. 'I think the gods are angry with us. We should return home. If we do not, harm may come to us.'

"'Let us rest by this knoll,' said one. 'When we have smoked, we will start back home.'

"They had smoked but one pipe when the leader said, 'I think we should go now. There is something strange about this knoll. Somehow, I think it is alive.'

"There was a young man in the party, reckless and full of life, whom the others called the Mocker. He sprang up crying, 'Let us see if it is alive. Come on, we will dance on the knoll.'

"'No,' said the leader, 'an evil spirit may be in the knoll. The hill may be but the spirit's body. It is not wise to mock the gods.'

"'*Hwee*[26]—come on! Who is afraid?' cried the Mocker. He ran to the top of the knoll, and three of the party followed him laughing. They leaped and danced and called to the others, 'What do you fear?'

[26] Hwēē

"Suddenly the knoll began to shake. It put out legs. It began to move toward the lake. It was a huge turtle.

"'Help, help!' cried the Mocker. He and his friends tried to escape. They could not. Some power held their feet fast to the turtle's back, so that they could not move.

"The great turtle plunged in the lake. The men were never seen again."

There was silence when Scar ended. Then Crow-Flies-High spoke: "Those men were foolish. One should never make mock of the spirits." He paused, puffing at his pipe and blowing great clouds from his nostrils. "I know a story of another Dakota who came to grief at a lake," he continued, as he passed the burning pipe for my husband to smoke.

"What is the story?" said Scar, smiling.

"We Hidatsas," said Crow-Flies-High, "believe that all babies born in our tribe have lived in another life. Some have lived in hills we call Babes' Lodges. Others have lived as birds or beasts or even plants.

"Down near the Dakota country is a lake. It is magic; and in old times young men went there to see what they had been in a former life. If one got up early in the morning while the lake was smooth, and looked in the water, he saw in his shadow the shadow also of what he had been. Some found this to be a bird, others a plant, as a flower or a squash.

"A Dakota Indian had married a Hidatsa woman, and dwelt with our tribe. He was a good man, but he had a sharp tongue. He often got angry and said bitter words to his wife. When his anger had gone, he felt sorry for his words. 'I do not know why I have such a sharp tongue,' he would say.

"One day, when hunting with some Hidatsas, he came near the magic lake. 'I am going to see what I was before I became a babe,' he told the others. In the morning he went to the lake, leaned over and looked. In his shadow he saw what he had been. It was a thorn bush.

"With heavy heart, he came back to camp. 'Now I know why I have a sharp tongue,' he cried. 'It is because I was a thorn bush. All my life I shall speak sharp words, like thorns.'"

All laughed at Crow-Flies-High's story, none more than Scar himself. "I am sure *I* was never a thorn bush," he said, "for I speak sweet words to my wife, even when she scolds me."

"Hey, listen to the man!" cried his wife.

"But stop talking, you men," she continued, as she reached for a piece of bark to use as a shovel. "It is time to sleep, for we must be up early in the morning." And she began to cover the fire with ashes.

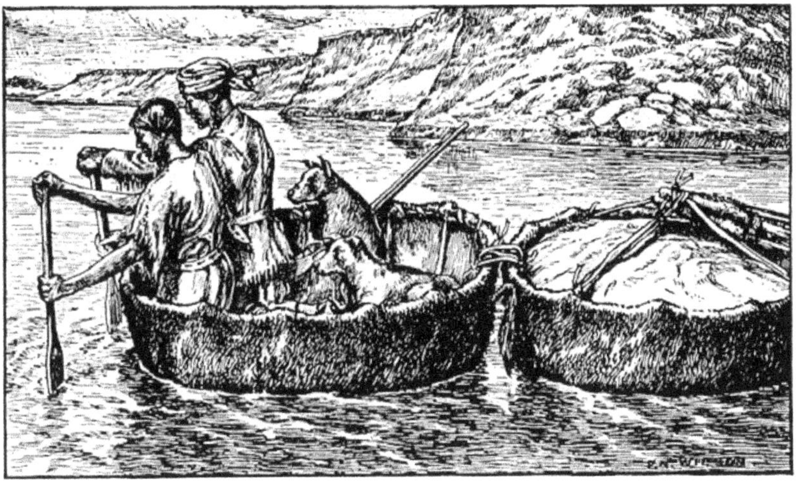

FIFTEENTH CHAPTER

THE HUNTING CAMP

We were up the next morning before the sun, and, after a hasty breakfast, the men went out to look for buffaloes. "The one we killed yesterday may have strayed from a herd," Son-of-a-Star said. He was hopeful that they might find the herd near.

We women were getting dinner when the men returned, having seen no buffaloes. I had cut a green stick with prongs, on which I spread slices of fresh buffalo steak, and held them over the fire to broil. I had three juicy steaks, steaming hot, lying on a little pile of clean grass, when my husband came in. "*Sukkeets*—good!" he cried; and he had eaten all three steaks before I had the fourth well warmed through.

After dinner we broke camp and went on about five miles to Shell Creek Lake. In the afternoon of the following day we reached Deep Creek. We pitched our tent on a bit of rising ground from which we scraped the wet snow with a hoe. The weather was getting warmer. Ice had broken on the Missouri the day we killed the stray buffalo.

While we women busied ourselves with things in camp, the men went to hunt, and five miles farther on they discovered a herd of buffaloes crossing the Missouri from the south side. Our hunters, creeping close on the downwind side, shot five fat cows as they landed. Buffaloes are rather stupid animals, but have keen scent. Had our hunters tried to come at them from the windward side, the herd would have winded them a half mile away. As it was, no more buffaloes crossed after the shots were fired, and some that were in the water swam back to the other side. A rifle shot at the Missouri's edge will echo between the bluffs like a crash of thunder.

The hunters found an elm tree with low hanging branches, and under it they built a rude stage. Meat and skins of the slain buffaloes they laid on the floor of the stage, out of reach of wolves. Some of the meat they hung on the branches of the elm.

Son-of-a-Star brought back two hams and a tongue. I sliced the tough outer meat from the hams, to feed to my dogs. The bones, with the tender, inner meat, I laid on stones, around the fireplace, to roast, turning them now and then to keep the meat from scorching. The roasted meat we stripped off, and cracked the hot bones for the rich, yellow marrow.

The next morning Crow-Flies-High called a council, and we decided to cross over to the other side of the river. "The main herd is there," said

Crow-Flies-High. "We should hunt the buffaloes before they move to other pasture." We thought he spoke wisely, and men and women seized axes to cut a road through the willows for our travois.

These we now loaded. The dogs dragged them to the water's edge and we made ready to cross. There were two other bull boats in the party besides my own.

My husband helped me load my boat, and we pushed off, our three dogs swimming after us. We had bound our travois to the tail of the boat, one upon the other. The long runners dragged in the water, but the travois baskets, raised to the boat's edge, were hardly wetted.

We landed, and I lent my boat to Scar to bring over his wife and her camp stuff. Our whole party crossed and brought over their goods in two trips.

We packed our goods up the bank and made camp. While we women were cutting poles for our tent, we heard the men disputing. They were seated in a circle near our pile of goods. High Backbone had lighted a pipe.

"I say we should go across the river and get the meat we staged yesterday," said Crow-Flies-High. Others said, "No, there is better hunting on this side. Let us go at once and find the herd." And all took their guns and hastened off but High Backbone, who stayed to guard the camp. We were afraid enemies might also be following the herd.

But the hunters returned at evening without having seen buffalo sign, and hungry—so hungry that they ate up half our store of meat. After supper, Crow-Flies-High called them to another council. "I told you we should get the meat we staged," he said. "The gods gave us that meat. We should not waste it."

We recrossed the river the next morning and fetched back most of the staged meat and skins, reaching camp again in the early part of the afternoon. Too busy to stop and eat, we spent the rest of the day building stages and staking out the green hides to dry.

The next day we found to our joy that the wind had shifted to the west. Our stages were now hung with slices of drying meat, and we had built slow fires beneath. An east wind would have carried the smoke toward the herd and stampeded it.

It was evening and getting dusk when Son-of-a-Star came into the tent, saying, "Buffaloes are on a bluff a quarter of a mile up the river. I can see them moving against the sky line." We listened and heard the bulls roaring; so we knew a herd was coming in.

We were careful to chop no wood that evening, nor do anything to make noise. We smothered our fires, and we fed our dogs; for, with gorged stomachs, they would be sleepy and not bark. If a dog stirred in the night, one of us went out and quieted him.

We made another crossing the next morning to fetch over the last of the meat we had staged. We returned about noon. The first woman to climb the bank under our camp was Scar's wife, Blossom. She dropped her pack and came running back, her hands at each side of her head with two fingers crooked, like horns, the sign for buffaloes.

We hastened into camp and saw the buffaloes a quarter of a mile away, swarming over a bluff. There was a bit of bad-land formation below, round-topped buttes with grassy stretches between. In these lower levels the sun had started the grass, and I think the buffaloes were coming down into them to seek pasture.

Our hunters had come up from the boats, guns in hand, and set off at once, creeping up the coulees from the lee side, that the buffaloes might not wind them. Presently I saw a flash and a puff of smoke; then another, and another; and the reports came echoing down the river basin, *poh—poh—poh—poh, poh, poh!* like thunder, away off. The herd took to their heels. Buffaloes, when alarmed, usually run up-wind; but, as the wind had shifted again to the east, this would have taken the herd into the river; so they swerved off and went tearing away toward the north.

The hunters returned before evening. Son-of-a-Star was the first to come in. "I shot two fat cows," he cried. "I have cut up the meat and put it in a pile, covered with the skins." He had brought back the choice cuts, however, the tongues, kidneys and hams. We ate the kidneys raw.

In the morning we harnessed our dogs and went out to the butchering place. As we neared my husband's meat pile, I saw that he had driven a stick into the ground and tied his headcloth to it, like a flag. This was to keep away the wolves. There were many of them in the Missouri-river country then.

While the flag fluttered and they winded the human smell, wolves would not touch the meat pile.

Sometimes in the fall, when hunters were cutting up a dead buffalo, I have seen wolves, coyotes, and foxes, a half hundred maybe, stalking about or seated just out of bow shot, awaiting the time the hunters left. All then rushed in to gorge on the offal. The wolves often snarled and bit at one another as they ate.

re great thieves; but the kit foxes, I think, were boldest. ...ting party, sleeping at night in a tent, when I awoke, ...am. A kit fox had stolen into the tent and walked ...of one of the sleeping women. She was terribly vexed. ...stepped his foot in my mouth," she cried angrily. In the ...found the fox had made off with some of our meat.

...-a-Star uncovered his meat pile, and helped me load our travois, ...ding each load to its basket with thongs. By long use I knew how heavy a load each of my dogs was able to drag. When I thought the travois held enough, I lifted its poles and tried the weight with my hands.

My husband and I packed loads on our own backs. Mine, I remember, was a whole green buffalo cow skin, a side of ribs and a tongue. This was a heavy load for a woman, and my husband scolded me roundly when we came in to camp. "That is foolish," he said. "You will hurt your back." I liked to work, however, and I wanted to show the older women how much I could carry.

We remained in the camp about ten days. The men would hunt until they made a kill. Then we harnessed our dogs, and all went out to fetch in the meat. To do this took us about half a day. At other times, when not drying meat, we women busied ourselves making bull boats, to freight our meat down the river.

I have said that I had brought one boat up from the village on one of my dogs. I now made another. There were some *mahoheesha* willows growing near the camp. I made the boat frame of these, covering it with the green hide of a buffalo cow. *Mahoheesha* willows are light, tough, and bend to any shape. They make good boat ribs.

When ready to move camp, I carried my new boat down to the river, turned over my head like a big hat. At the water's edge I drove a stout stake into the mud, and to this I fastened the floating boat with a short thong.

Skins and dried meat had been made up into small bales. I packed these to the boat on my back, using a two-banded packing strap. As the river was not far from our camp and the bank not very steep, I did not think this task a hard one.

When the boat was filled, I covered the load neatly with a piece of old tent skin, and to the tail of the boat, I lashed my three travois. The buffalo skin covering a bull boat was so laid that the tail was to the rear of the boat. For this reason we often spoke of the boat's *head* and *tail*.

Meanwhile, Son-of-a-Star fetched the boat I had brought up from the village, and I bound it to the head of my newer boat. We were now ready to embark. I waded out, climbed into the empty, or passenger, boat, and called to my dogs. They leaped in beside me.

Son-of-a-Star took off his moccasins and rolled up his leggings. He handed me his gun, loosed the thong that bound the boats to the stake, pushed the boats into deeper water, and climbed in. I handed him his paddle.

I had hewn this paddle from a cottonwood log, only the day before. My own, lighter and better made, I had brought with me from the village. Each paddle had a large hole cut in the center of the blade. Without this hole, a paddle wobbled in the current.

On the front of my paddle blade, Son-of-a-Star had painted a part of his war record, hoof prints as of a pony, and moccasin tracks such as a man makes with his right foot. Hoof and footprints had each a wound mark, as of flowing blood. Son-of-a-Star had drawn these marks with his finger, dipped in warm buffalo fat and red ochre.

The marks were for a brave deed of my husband. He once rode against a party of Sioux, firing his gun, when a bullet went through his right thigh, and killed his horse. The footprints with the wound marks meant that Son-of-a-Star had been shot in his right leg.

On his own paddle my husband had marked a cross within bars. These meant, "I was one of four warriors to count *strike* on an enemy."

It was an Indian custom to mark a warrior's honors, much as a soldier wears stripes for the wounds he has had. I was quite proud of the marks on my paddles. I was a young woman, remember, and I thought, "Not every woman has a husband as brave as mine."

Just before I got into my boat I had paused to wash my sweaty face in the river, and, with a little ochre and buffalo fat, I painted my cheeks a bright red. I thought this made me look handsome; and, too, the paint kept my face from being tanned by the sun, for I had a light skin. In those days everybody painted, and came to feasts with handsome faces, red or yellow. Now we follow white men's ways, and we go about with faces pale, like ghosts from the Dead village. I think that is why some tribes call white men *pale-faces*; because they do not paint and are pale like ghosts.

Altogether there were eleven boats in our fleet, two to each couple except Scar and his wife, who had but one. At that, their one boat was enough, for they had small store of meat or skins to take home. They were a young couple and thought more of having a good time than of doing any hard work.

We had launched our boats in a tiny bay, and our paddles, dipping into the quiet backwater, sent the waves rippling against the shore. It was a crisp spring morning, and the sun, rising almost in our faces, threw a broad band of gold over the water. In the shadow of the opposite bank, a pelican was fishing. He paused to gaze at us, his yellow beak laid against his white plumage; then calmly went to fishing again. Out in mid-current, an uprooted tree swept by, and our skin boats, as they swung out of the bay, passed a deadhead that bobbed up and down, up and down. Then with a roar, the current caught us and bore us swiftly away.

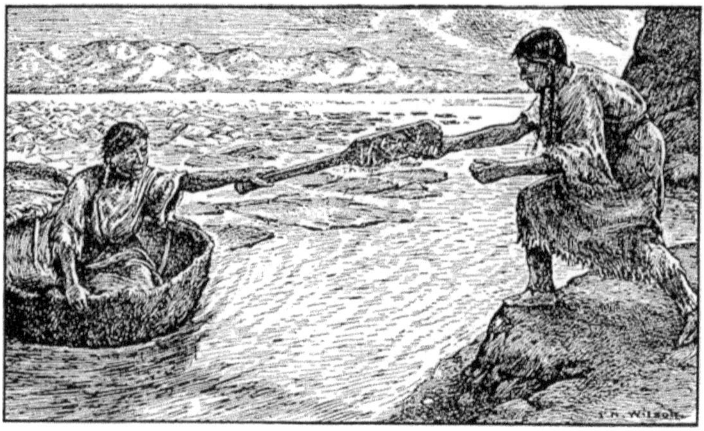

SIXTEENTH CHAPTER

HOMEWARD BOUND

When using her bull boat to cross over the river, a woman knelt in the bow and dipped her paddle in front of her; but, with a second and freighted boat in tow, my husband and I paddled, seated one at each side of our boat. We had not much need to use our paddles as long as we rode the current.

Crow-Flies-High led the way. We had gone, I think, an hour or two, and Crow-Flies-High's boat was rounding a point, when I saw him rise to his knees and back water with his paddle. My husband and I speeded up; and, as we came near, Crow-Flies-High pointed to the bank just below the point. It was thickly covered with buffaloes.

Scar's wife put her hand to her mouth for astonishment, but made no sound. If buffaloes have not good sight, they have keen ears; and she knew better than to cry out.

A bit of woodland stretched along the shore farther on. Crow-Flies-High signed for us to follow, and we floated silently down to the end of the woods, where the trees hid us from the herd. The men sprang out and held the boats while we women landed.

The bank was high and rather steep, but at its foot was a narrow bench of sand a foot or more above the water's level. We hastily unloaded our boats and dragged them out upon this sand.

Along the Missouri's edge are always to be found dead-and-dry willow sticks, left there by the falling current. I gathered an armful of these, and, having climbed the bank, laid them together in a kind of floor. Son-of-a-Star now helped me fetch up our bundles, and we piled them on this willow floor. He also brought up my two boats. These I turned, bottom up, over my pile of bundles, to keep off frost and rain.

The men now seized their guns and hastened off after the buffaloes. It was about noon. I think we had spent less than an hour unloading the boats and packing them and our stuff to the top of the bank.

While our hunters were stalking the herd, we women stayed in camp, keeping very quiet, and stilling the dogs if they whined or barked. Before long we heard the *poh-poh-poh!* of guns, and knew the herd was started. We now arose and began gathering sticks for a fire. I think the first man to return struck fire for us, and we got dinner.

We did not trouble to set up our tent. "The weather is not cold," said Crow-Flies-High's wife. "We can sleep in the open air." I cut buck-brush bushes and spread a robe over them for my bed. Dry grass stuffed under one end of the robe did for a pillow. My covering was a pair of buffalo skins. We were weary and went to bed early. The night was clear; and, with the fresh river air blowing in my face, I soon fell asleep.

We were astir the next morning at an early hour. While Son-of-a-Star started a fire, I went to fill my copper kettle at the river. My husband had asked me to boil him some meat, for the broth; for in old times we Indians drank broth instead of coffee.

The river's roar, I thought, sounded louder than usual; and, when I reached the edge of the high bank, I saw that the current was thronged with masses of ice. This amazed me, for the river had been running free for a fortnight. The Missouri is never a silent stream, and now to the roar of its waters was added the groaning and crashing of the ice cakes, as they grated and pounded one another in the current.

When the Missouri is running ice, the mid-current will be thronged, well-nigh choked, with ice masses, but near the banks, where are shallows, the water will be free, since here the stream is not deep enough to float the ice chunks. On the side of the river under our camp was a margin of ice-free water of this kind; and I now saw, out near the edge of the floating ice, two bull boats bound together, with a woman in the foremost, paddling with all her might. She was struggling to keep from being caught in the ice and crushed.

I ran down the bank to the bench of sand below, just as the boats came sweeping by. The woman saw me and held out her paddle crying, "Daughter, save me!" I seized the wet blade, and tugging hard, drew the boats to shore. The woman was *Amaheetseekuma*,[27] or Lies-on Red-Hill, a woman older than I, and my friend.

[27] A mä hēēt´ sēē kụ mä

Lies-on-Red-Hill, though rather fat, scrambled quickly out of the boat and began tumbling her bundles out upon the sand. The other women of our party now came down, and we helped my friend carry her bundles up to the camp.

As we sat by the fire, wringing and drying her moccasins, Lies-on-Red-Hill told us her story: "My husband, Short Bull, and I were hunting buffaloes. We dried much meat, which I loaded in my two boats, to freight down the river. While I paddled, Short Bull was to go along the shore with our horses. 'We will meet at Beaver Wood,' he said, 'and camp.' But I did not find him at Beaver Wood. Then ice came. I was afraid to camp alone, and tried to paddle down stream, keeping near the shore, where was no ice. More ice came, and I feared I should be upset and drown."

It was not until afterwards, when we reached our village, that we learned why Short Bull did not meet his wife. He got to Beaver Wood ahead of her. Not finding her, and thinking she had passed him, he went on to the place where they had agreed to make their second camping. When again she did not come, he became alarmed, and returned up the river looking for her. In the morning he saw the river was full of ice. "She is drowned," he thought. And he went on to Like-a-Fishhook village.

Lies-on-Red-Hill's father was an old man named Dried Squash. He was fond of his daughter, and, when he heard she was drowned, he put her squash basket on his back and went through the village weeping and crying out, "Lies-on-Red-Hill, dear daughter, I shall never see you again." He wanted to leap into the river and die, but his friends held him.

Lies-on-Red-Hill rested in our camp two days. The third morning the river was running free again, and she loaded her boats and paddled off down stream. The rest of us stayed one more day, to finish drying and packing our meat. Then we, too, loaded our boats and started down the river.

We floated with the current, and the second day sighted Stands-Alone Point, or Independence, as white men now call it. Here a party of Mandans were just quitting camp. They pushed their boats into the current and caught up with us. "We knew you were coming," they said. "Lies-on-Red-Hill told us. She passed us yesterday."

Our united party floated safely down until we were two miles below what is now Elbowoods. Here, to our astonishment, we found that the current was hardly running, and the water was backing up and flooding the shores. We rounded a point of land, and saw what was the matter. Ice, brought down on the current, had jammed, bridging the river and partly damming it.

Fearing to go farther, we were bringing our boats to land, when we heard the sound of a gun and voices calling to us. On the opposite shore stood two white men, waving handkerchiefs.

We paddled across and landed. The white men, we found, were traders, who had married Indian women. They had a flat boat, loaded with buffalo skins and furs. With them was Lies-on-Red-Hill. One of the traders we Indians had named Spots, because he had big freckles on his face.

Like-a-Fishhook village was yet about fifteen miles away. While the rest of our party waited, one of the men went afoot, to notify our relatives. They came about noon, the next day, with ponies and saddles to help us bring home our goods. The saddles were pack saddles, made with horn frames.

It took four ponies to pack the dried meat and skins my husband and I had brought. I loaded my boats on the travois of two of my dogs.

We reached Like-a-Fishhook village at sunset. Lies-on-Red-Hill came with us, to the great joy of her father.

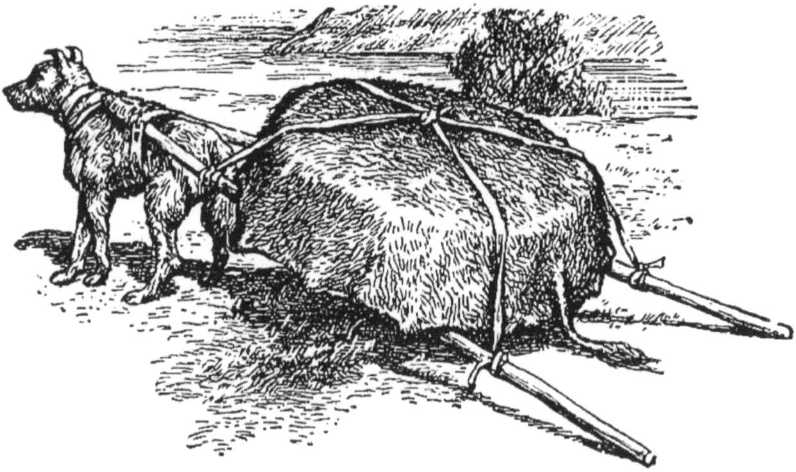

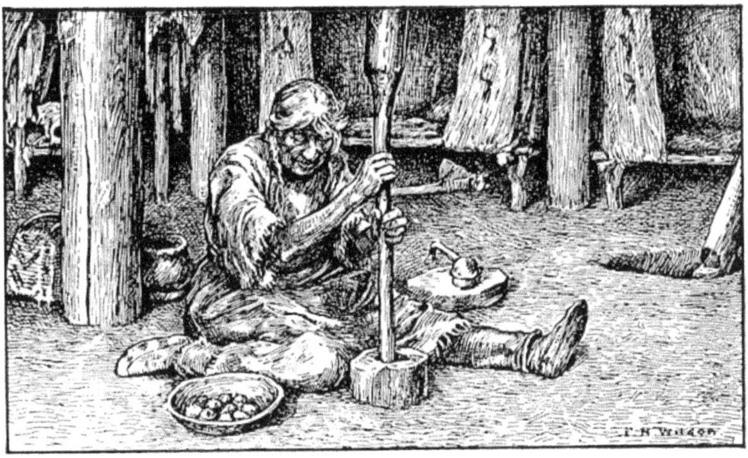
I. N. Wilson

SEVENTEENTH CHAPTER

AN INDIAN PAPOOSE

My father was overjoyed to see me and my husband again, and he was glad for the store of meat that we brought. We had a real feast the next day. I boiled green corn, shelled from the cob and dried the summer before, and packed away in skin bags. We were fond of this corn, and had little of it left. Strikes-Many Woman parched ripe sweet corn, pounded it in a mortar with roast buffalo fats, and kneaded the meal into little balls.

With these corn messes and boiled dried buffalo meat we made a big feast and called in all our relatives. To each woman guest, as she went away again, I gave a bundle of dried buffalo meat; and I thus gave away one of the four pony-loads of meat I had brought home. It was an Indian custom that, when a hunter brought in meat of a deer or buffalo, it belonged to his wife; and we should have thought her a bad woman, if she did not feast her relatives and give to them.

My father sat with his cronies at the right of the fireplace, at our feast. We women ate apart, for men and women do not sit together at an Indian feast. I heard my father talking with his friend, Lean Wolf: "Every spring, when I was young, we fired the prairie grass around the Five Villages. Green grass then sprang up; buffaloes came to graze on it, and we killed many."

"Those were good days," said Lean Wolf. "There were many buffaloes then."

"It is so," said my father. "It is now seven years since a herd was seen near our village. White men's guns have driven them away. And each year we kill fewer deer."

"I have heard that some Sioux families starved last winter," said Lean Wolf.

"They starved, because they are hunters and raise no corn," said my father. "We Hidatsas must plant more corn, or we shall starve; and we must learn to raise white men's wheat and potatoes." Small Ankle was a progressive old man.

One morning, not long after our feast, Red Blossom came in from the woods with news that the wild gooseberry vines were in leaf. This was a sign that corn planting time was come, and we women began to make ready our corn seed and sharpen our hoes.

I had been thinking of my father's words to Lean Wolf. "They are wise words," I told my mothers. "We should widen our fields, and plant more corn." While they busied themselves with planting, I worked with my hoe around the edges of our two fields, breaking new ground.

Having thus more ground to work over, my mothers planted for more than a month, or well into June. The last week of our planting, Red Blossom soaked her corn seed in tepid water. "It will make the seed sprout earlier," she said, "so that the ears will ripen before frost comes."

Our fall harvest was good. My two mothers and I were more than a week threshing and winnowing our corn; but some families, less wise than ours, had not increased their planting, and had none too much grain to lay by for winter. This troubled our chief men. "The summer's hunt has been poor," they said. "If our winter's hunting is not better, we shall be hungry before harvest comes again."

They had twice called a council to talk of the matter, when scouts brought word that buffaloes had been seen. "Big herds have come down into the Yellowstone country," they said. The Black Mouths thought we should make our winter camp there, in tepees; and they went about choosing a winter chief.

But no one wanted to be winter chief. Camping in the Yellowstone country in skin tents, was not like our wintering in earth lodges in the woods near our village. The people expected their chief's prayers to keep enemies away and bring them good hunting. If ill luck came to any in the camp, they blamed the winter chief.

The Black Mouths offered gifts to one or another of our chief men, whose prayers we knew were strong; but none would take them. At last, they gave half the gifts to *Eydeeahkata*,[28] and half to Short Horn. "You shall take turns at being chief," they said. "*Eydeeahkata* shall lead one day and Short Horn the next."

[28] Ey dēē äh´ kä tä

The two leaders chose Red Kettle to be their crier. The evening before we started he went through the village crying, "We move to-morrow at sunrise. Get ready."

Our way led up the Missouri, above the bluffs; and most of the time we were within sight of the river. Now and then, if the current made a wide bend, we took a shorter course over the prairie. *Eydeeahkata* and Short Horn went ahead, each with a sacred medicine bundle bound to his saddle bow. The camp followed in a long line. Some rode ponies, but most went afoot. We camped at night in our tepees.

We made our eleventh camp on the north side of the Missouri, a few miles below the mouth of the Yellowstone. Here the Missouri is not very wide, and its sloping banks make a good place for crossing. A low bank of clean, hard sand lay along the water's edge. We pitched our tents about noon on this sand. There were about a hundred tepees. They stood in rows, like houses, for there was not room on the sand to make a camping circle.

Small Ankle pitched his tent near the place chosen for the crossing. The day was windy and chill. With flint-and-steel my father struck a fire, and we soon had meat boiling. After our dinner he drove his horses to pasture.

Strikes-Many Woman fetched dry grass for our beds, spreading it thickly on the floor against the tent wall. On the edges of the beds next the fireplace she laid small logs, to keep in the grass bedding and to catch any flying sparks from the fire.

The wind died at evening. Twilight fell, and the coals in the fireplace cast a soft, red glow on the tent walls. I sat near the tent door. With robe drawn over my shoulders to keep off the chill, I raised the skin door and looked out. The new moon, narrow and bent like an Indian bow, shone white over the river, and the waves of the swift mid-current sparkled silvery in the moonlight. I could hear the swish of eddies, the lap-lapping of the waves rolling shoreward. Over all rose the roar, roar, roar of the great river, sweeping onward we Indians knew not where.

Plate III.—"With horn spoon she filled her mouth with water."

My dogs were sleeping without, snugged against the tent for warmth. At midnight one of them stirred, pointed his nose at the moon and broke into a howl. The howl soon grew to a chorus, for every dog in the camp joined in. Far out on the prairie rose the wailing *yip-yip-yip-yip-ya-a-ah!*[29] of a coyote. The dogs grew silent again, and curled up, nose-in-tail, to sleep.

[29] yĭp yĭp yĭp yĭp yä´ ä äh

And my little son came into the world.

The morning sky was growing light when Son-of-a-Star came into the tent. His eyes were smiling as he stepped to the fireplace, for they saw a pretty sight. Red Blossom was giving my baby a bath.

She had laid him on a piece of soft skin, before the fire. With horn spoon she filled her mouth with water, held it in her cheeks until it was warm, and blew it over my baby's body. I do not think he liked his bath, for he squalled loudly.

My husband laughed. "It is a lusty cry," he said. "I am sure my son will be a warrior."

Having bathed my baby, Red Blossom bound him in his wrapping skins. She had a square piece of tent cover, folded and sewed along the edges of one end into a kind of sack. Into this she slipped my baby, with his feet against the sewed end. About his little body she packed cattail down.

On a piece of rawhide, she put some clean sand, which she heated by rolling over it a red-hot stone. She packed this sand under my baby's feet; and, lest it prove too hot, she slipped a piece of soft buckskin under them.

Over all she bound a wildcat skin, drawing the upper edge over the baby's head, like a hood.

The hot sand was to keep my baby warm. This and the cattail down we placed in a baby's wrappings only in winter, when on a journey.

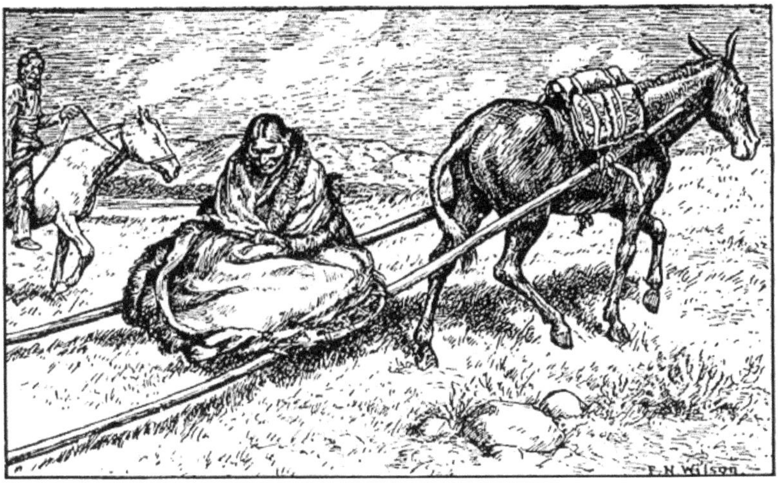
E. N. Wilson

EIGHTEENTH CHAPTER

THE VOYAGE HOME

Meanwhile Small Ankle and other members of the family were making ready to cross. "We must hasten," my father said. "Ice chunks are running on the current this morning. This shows that up in the mountains the river is freezing over and cold weather is setting in."

My mothers began packing soon after breakfast and Son-of-a-Star came in to say that he would take me across in our bull boat; for we had brought one with us from the village. Old Turtle began unpinning the tent cover while I was still inside. She made the tent poles into a bundle and bound them at the tail of the boat. I stepped in with my baby in my arms and my husband paddled the boat across.

Son-of-a-Star helped me up the bank on the other side and gave me a place to sit where I could watch the crossing. I folded a robe to sit upon, and, with another robe drawn snugly over my shoulders and my baby in my arms, I felt comfortable and warm.

My husband even made a small fire in a hollow place in the ground near-by. One of my women friends boiled some meat and gave me the hot broth to drink; for I was weary with the work of crossing and caring for my babe.

There were not enough boats in the camp for all the people. Most of the old people and little children were brought over in boats, and some of the camp goods; but many families floated their stuff over in tent covers, and, cold as was the water, many of the men swam.

I had left my two mothers and old Turtle loading their tent cover. Turtle had made a big noose in the end of a lariat and laid it on the sand. Over this she spread the skin cover, a large one. She bent a green willow into a hoop, laid it on the tent cover, and within the hoop piled most of our camp goods. She now gathered the edges of the cover together over the pile, drew tight the noose, and tied it firm. This tent-cover bundle my mothers and old Turtle pushed out into the water as a kind of raft. The willow hoop gave the raft a flat bottom so that it did not turn over in the water.

The lariat that bound the mouth of the raft was fastened to the tail of a pony we had named Shaggy, and the end was carried into and about the pony's mouth like a halter. Shaggy was driven into the stream and swam across, towing the raft. The lariat was fastened to his tail so that, if the raft was swept down stream by the current, it would not drag the pony's head, and turn him from his course.

As I have said, many families floated their goods over in these tent-cover rafts; and not a few women, in haste to cross, swam clinging to their rafts. One woman put her little four-year-old son on the top of her raft, while she swam behind, pushing and guiding it. Another old woman, named Owl Ear, mounted her raft and rode astraddle. Her pony landed in a place where the shore was soft with oozy mud, so that he could not climb out. Owl Ear had to wade in the mud up to her middle to get her raft ashore; and when she was climbing out she slipped and sat down backwards again in the ooze. She came up sputtering mud from her mouth and much vexed with herself. "I think there must be bad spirits in that mud, and they are trying to pull me back," she called to me, as she came waddling up the steep bank.

Before evening my mothers had brought all their camp goods across. They raised the poles of our tent and drew on the cover. It was wet, but soon dried in the wind. We built a fire inside. My baby had wakened up and was crying. I loosened his wrapping and warmed him by the tent fire, and he soon fell asleep. Red Blossom dug a hole, slipped into it a kind of sack of raw hide, for a mortar. We had brought a pestle with us from the village, and with this we pounded parched corn to a meal to boil with beans. We ate a late supper and went to bed.

We camped on the bank three days, until all had crossed. Our chiefs would not remain longer, for they wanted to get into winter camp before snow fell; and, on the morning of the fourth day, we struck tents and made ready to march.

There was a mule in our family herd, a slow-going, gentle beast, that I had bought of a Sioux for a worthless pony and some strings of corn. Son-of-a-Star harnessed this mule to a travois, and my baby and I rode. Had our march been in olden days, I should have had to go afoot, carrying my baby on my back.

My husband had spread a heavy bull-skin robe over the travois basket and set me on it, with another skin folded under me for a cushion. Through holes in the edge of the bull skin Son-of-a-Star passed a lariat; and when I was seated, with my baby in my arms and my robe belted snugly about us, my husband drew the lariat, drawing the bull skin about my knees and ankles. The day was windy and cold, and the bull skin kept the chill air from me and my babe.

Our leaders had chosen for our winter camp a place called Round Bank, on a small stream named Bark Creek. There were no trees here for building earth lodges, so we camped in our tepees, pitching them in a hollow, to shelter them from the wind. The ground was frozen so that we could not peg our tents to the ground, but laid stones around the edges of the tent covers. Such was our older-fashioned way. We did not use wooden tent pegs much until after we got iron axes.

My mothers fetched dry grass into our tent for our beds, and made a fire under the smoke hole. A tepee was kept warm with a rather small fire, if it was well sheltered from the wind.

Ours was a big tent, for we had a big family. With my two half brothers, Bear's Tail and Wolf Chief, and their wives; and Red Kettle, Full House, and Flies Low, younger sons of Red Blossom and Strikes-Many Woman, we numbered fourteen in all. This was a large number for one tent. Ten were as many as a tepee usually sheltered. Every member of the family had his own bed, where he slept at night and sat in the daylight hours.

My little son was ten days old the second day we were in winter camp; and, though we were hardly well settled, I found time to make ready his naming feast. Having filled a wooden bowl with venison and boiled dried green corn—foods I knew well were to his liking—I set it before Small Ankle.

"I want you to name your grandson," I said to him.

Small Ankle ate, thinking the while what name he should give my son. Then he arose and took my baby tenderly in his arms, saying, "I name him *Tsakahka Sukkee*,[30] Good Bird." Small Ankle's gods were birds, and the name was a kind of prayer that they remember and help my little son.

[30] Tsä käh´ kä Sŭk´ kēē

Winter passed without mishap to us. We had found no buffaloes on the Yellowstone; but our hunters thrice discovered small herds near our camp and brought in meat; and a good many deer were killed.

Rather early in the spring, the women of the Goose Society danced and hung up meat for the goose spirits, praying them for good weather for corn planting. Then we all broke camp.

Most of the tribe returned to the Yellowstone for the spring hunt, but my father wanted to go up the Missouri. "We have not found the herds our scouts saw in the fall," he said. "I am sure they are farther up the river."

One Buffalo and his family joined us and we went up the river and made camp. A small herd was sighted and ten buffaloes were killed.

We were building stages to dry the meat when four more tents caught up with us, those of Strikes Backbone, Old Bear, Long Wing, and Spotted Horn, and their families. To each tent owner my father gave a whole green buffalo hide and a side of meat. The hides were for making bull boats, for we were planning to return home by water.

Ice broke on the Missouri and flocks of wild ducks began coming north. My mothers were eager to be home in time for the spring planting. I made four new boats, giving one of them to my father, and we made ready to go.

Son-of-a-Star partly loaded one of my boats with dried meat, and put in his gun and ax. A second boat, also partly loaded, he lashed to the first; and a third, loaded to the gunwale with meat and hides, he bound to the tail of the second. In this second boat sat my half brother, Flies Low, a seventeen-year-old lad, with my baby in his arms. My husband and I sat in the first boat and paddled.

There were eleven boats in the six families of our party. One or two families, having no meat to freight, rode in single boats. My father and two of the men did not come in the boats, but rode along the bank, driving our horses. They kept back near the foot hills, but in sight of the river.

We were in no haste, and we made a jolly party as we floated down the broad current. At night we paddled to the shore. The men joined us with the horses, and we camped under the stars.

The Missouri is a swift stream, and at places we found the waves were quite choppy. Especially if a bend in the river carried the current against the wind, the waves rolled and foamed, rocking our boats and threatening to swamp us. At such times we drew together, catching hold of one another's boats. Thus bunched, our fleet rode the choppy current more safely than a single boat could have done.

The weather had set in rather warm when we left our winter camp and the grass had already begun to show green on the prairie. But, as we neared the mouth of the Little Missouri, a furious storm of snow and wind arose. The storm blew up suddenly, and, as we rounded a bend in the river, we rode into the very teeth of the wind.

Son-of-a-Star shouted to me to turn in to the shore, though I could hardly hear his voice above the wind. We plied our paddles with all our might.

Suddenly my husband stopped paddling and leaned over the side of the boat, nigh upsetting it. "*Eena, eena*"[31] I cried, scared nearly out of my wits, and I grasped at the boat's edge to keep from being tumbled in upon him. Then I saw what was the matter. My husband was lifting my little son out of the water.

[31] ēē nä´

I have said that Flies Low sat in our second boat, with my little son in his arms. The baby had grown restless, and Flies Low had loosened the babe's wrappings to give freedom of his limbs. A sudden billow rocked the boat, throwing Flies Low against the side and tumbling my little son out of his arms into the water.

His loosened wrappings, by some good luck, made my baby buoyant, so that he floated. He was crying lustily when my husband drew him out; but he was not strangling, and under his wraps he was not even wet.

"I could not help it," said Flies Low afterwards. "The boat seemed to turn over, and the baby fell out of my arms." We knew this was true and said nothing more of it.

Our party reached shore without further mishap. We hastily unpacked two tents; and, while some busied themselves pitching them, others gathered wood and made fires.

That night the snow turned to a cold rain, which the next day turned again into a heavy snow. The summer birds had come north, and after the storm was over we found many of them frozen to death. It snowed for four days.

Small Ankle and his brother, Charging Enemy, were driving their horses along the bank when the storm overtook them. They did not stop to camp with us, but pushed on through the storm to Like-a-Fishhook village. They reached the village safely and drove their horses down into the thick timber out of the cold wind. There was a pond there, and the horses found it warmer to wade out into the water than to stand on the bank in the cold rain. But after a while, grown weary with standing, they came out; and, as the wind was blowing a gale, the horses were chilled and three of them died. Many others of our village herd died in the same way.

Our own party, as soon as the storm was over, re-embarked and floated safely down to Like-a-Fishhook village.

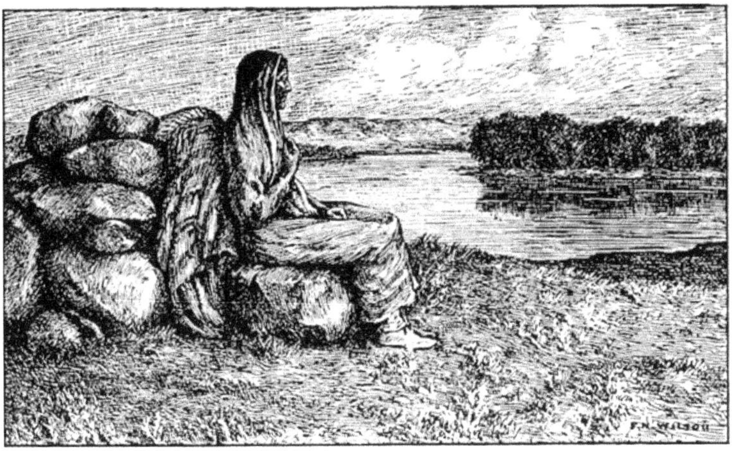

AFTER FIFTY YEARS

I am an old woman now. The buffaloes and black-tail deer are gone, and our Indian ways are almost gone. Sometimes I find it hard to believe that I ever lived them.

My little son grew up in the white man's school. He can read books, and he owns cattle and has a farm. He is a leader among our Hidatsa people, helping teach them to follow the white man's road.

He is kind to me. We no longer live in an earth lodge, but in a house with chimneys; and my son's wife cooks by a stove.

But for me, I cannot forget our old ways.

Often in summer I rise at daybreak and steal out to the cornfields; and as I hoe the corn I sing to it, as we did when I was young. No one cares for our corn songs now.

Sometimes at evening I sit, looking out on the big Missouri. The sun sets, and dusk steals over the water. In the shadows I seem again to see our Indian village, with smoke curling upward from the earth lodges; and in the river's roar I hear the yells of the warriors, the laughter of little children as of old. It is but an old woman's dream. Again I see but shadows and hear only the roar of the river; and tears come into my eyes. Our Indian life, I know, is gone forever.

GLOSSARY OF INDIAN WORDS

English equivalents are in italics

Ä hä hey´	An exclamation; *Ho there!*
Ä hä hu̱ts´	*They come against us.*
Ä kēē´ kä hēē	*Took-from-Him*; name of a dog.
Ä lä lä lä lä´	Cry of triumph by women; made by curling the tip of the tongue backward and vibrating it against the roof of the mouth.
Ä mä hēēt´ sēē ku̱ mä	*Lies-on-Red-Hill*; name of a woman.
Ēē´ ku̱ pä	*Chum.*
Ēē nä´	An exclamation.
Ēēt sēē pä däh´ pä kēē	*Foot moving*; name of a game.
Ēēt su̱´ tä	Name of the large tendon of a buffalo's neck.
E̱y	An exclamation.
E̱y dēē äh´ kä tä	Name of an Indian.
Hau (how)	The Indian salutation.
He̱y dä ey´	An exclamation of pleasure.
Hwēē	*Hasten*; an exclamation.
Mä hō´ hēē shä	A species of willow.
Mä ku̱t´ sä tēē	*Clan cousin.*
Mä pēē´	*Meal made by pounding.*
Mä pu̱k´ sä ō	*Snake Head-Ornament*; a man's name.

kĭ hĕ

Mēē dä´ hēē kä	*Gardeners' songs.*
Mēē dēē päh´ dēē	*Rising water*; name of a Hidatsa clan, or band.
Näh	*Go, come.*
Nä kä päh´	*Mush.*
O kēē mēē´ ä	*Head-Ornament Woman*; a woman's name.
Shēē´ pēē shä	*Black.*
Sŭk´ kēēts (or Sŭkkēē)	*Good.*
Tsä käh´ ka Sŭk´ kēē	Name of Waheenee's son; from *tsakahka*, bird, and *sukkee*, good.
Tsïst´ skä	*Prairie chicken.*
Ų´ ï	The Hidatsa war whoop.
Wä hēē´ nēē	*Cowbird*, or *Buffalo-bird*; name of the Indian woman whose story is told in this book.
Wē´ä	*Woman.*
Wų ų ų	Imitation of a dog's bark.
Yĭ yĭ yĭ yĭ yäh´	A war cry of triumph, made with hand vibrated over the mouth or against the throat.
Wē´ äh tēē	A woman's name.

EXPLANATORY NOTES

Page 9, l. 24: "We had corn a-plenty" The Hidatsas and Mandans were the best agriculturists of the north-plains Indians. Varieties of corn developed by them mature in the semi-arid climate of western North Dakota where our better known eastern strains will not ripen. The varieties include flint, flour, and a kind of sweet corn called *maikadishake*,[32] or gummy, which the Indians use for parching. Hidatsa seed planted at the United States Agricultural Experiment Station at Bozeman, Montana, has made surprising yields.

[32] mä´ ĭ kä dĭ shä kĕ

Page 10, l. 29: "the ghost land." A Hidatsa Indian believed he had four ghosts. At death, one ghost went to the Ghost village, to live in an earth lodge and hunt buffaloes as on earth; a second remained at the grave until after a time it joined the first in the Ghost village where they became one again. What became of the other two ghosts does not seem to be known.

Page 11, l. 20: "The march was led by the older chiefs." A Hidatsa chief was a man who by his war deeds, hospitality, and wisdom, came to be recognized as one of the influential men of the tribe. He was not necessarily an officer. When translating into English, Hidatsas usually call the officer elected for any executive duty a *leader*, as war-party leader, winter-camp leader, leader of the buffalo hunt. It should be remembered that the activities of an Indian tribe are decided in councils; and in these councils the eloquence and wisdom of the chiefs had greatest weight. The Hidatsa word for chief, literally translated, is excellent man, superior man.

Page 13, l. 8: "At this hour fires burned before most of the tepees." In fall or winter the fire was within the tepee, under the smoke hole.

Page 15, l. 13: "for a woman to ... begin building her earth lodge." While the work falling to an Indian woman was far from light, she did not look upon herself as overburdened. Women were more kindly treated by Hidatsas and Mandans than by some tribes.

Page 17, l. 28: "dried prairie turnips." The prairie turnip, *psoralea esculenta*, is a starchy, bulbous root, growing rather plentifully on the plains. Its food value is high. Attempts have been made unsuccessfully to cultivate it.

Page 17, l. 30: "June berries." The June berry, *amelanchier alnifolia*, is a small, hardwood tree, bearing sweet, dark-red berries. Its branches were much used for making arrow shafts.

Page 21, l. 14: "young men fasted and cut their flesh." Such self-inflicted tortures were not, as is often believed, for the purpose of proving the warrior's fortitude, but were made as a kind of sacrifice to the gods that these might pity the devotee and answer his prayers. See Bible, I Kings, XVIII; 28.

Page 24, l. 30: "It was a long pipe with black stone bowl." The stone bowl was carved from a hard kind of grey clay, anointed with grease and baked in a fire to turn it black. It took a high polish.

Page 35, l. 11: "Telling tales ... in ... autumn and winter." Tribal myths, told of the gods, were often forbidden in summer when nature was *alive*. In winter nature was *asleep* or *dead*. One could talk of sleeping spirits without fear of offending them.

Page 36, l. 5: "Making ready her seed." The Hidatsas used the greatest care in selecting their seed corn. Only large and perfect ears were chosen. The best ear for seed was the *eeteeshahdupadee*,[33] or muffled-head, so called because the kernels cover the cob quite to the tip, making the ear look like an Indian with his head muffled up in his robe.

[33] ēē tēē shä dụ´ pä dēē

Page 36, l. 14: "Wooden bowl." In olden days almost every family owned several of these feast bowls. A large knot was split out of a tree trunk with wedges and, after being hollowed out with fire, was slowly carved into shape with flint tools. Some of these bowls are beautiful examples of carving.

Page 37, l. 16: "Trying to parch an ear of corn." Parched corn entered largely into the diet of our corn raising Indians. Among eastern tribes, a warrior set forth on a long journey with a sack of parched corn pounded to a meal. When hungry, he swallowed a spoonful of the parched meal, washing it down with a pint of water. In a short time the meal had absorbed the water, filling the stomach with a digestible mass like mush.

Every farmer's lad should put away some ears of ripened sweet corn in the fall, to parch of a winter's evening. Sweet corn was raised by the Hidatsas and Mandans for parching only.

Page 38, l. 21: "Ground beans," or hog peanut; *amphicarpa falcata*. These beans, like peanuts, are borne under ground.

Page 38, l. 22: "Wild potatoes," or Jerusalem artichoke. Roots of *helianthus tuberosus*, a plant of the sunflower family.

Page 41, l. 25: "Who had been a black bear." Tradition has it that the art and mysteries of trapping eagles were taught the Hidatsas by the black bears. An eagle hunters' camp was conducted as a kind of symbolic play, the hunters acting the ceremonies of the delivery to the Indians of the eagle-hunt mysteries.

Page 44, l. 17: "Earth lodges well-built and roomy." The earth lodge of the Mandans and Hidatsas was the highest example of the building art among our plains tribes. Some of these lodges were quite large, having a height of eighteen feet or more, and a floor diameter exceeding sixty feet. Usually two or more families of relatives inhabited the same lodge.

An earth lodge had four large central posts and beams, supporting the roof; twelve surrounding posts and beams, supporting the eaves; and a hundred rafters. The roof was covered with a matting of willows over which was laid dry grass and a heavy coating of earth.

An earth lodge lasted but about ten years, when it was abandoned or rebuilt. The labor of building and repairing these imposing structures, especially in days when iron tools were unknown and posts and beams had to be burned to proper lengths, must have been severe.

When the author first visited Fort Berthold reservation in 1906, there were eight earth lodges still standing; in 1918 there were two.

Page 47, l. 18: "An earthen pot." The potter's craft was practiced professionally by certain women who had purchased the secrets of the art. The craft was an important one, as much of Hidatsa cooking was by boiling. Some of the earthen boiling pots held as much as two gallons. A collection of earthen pots, fired in 1910 by Hides-and-Eats, a Mandan woman nearly ninety years old, is in the American Museum of Natural History.

Page 49, l. 18: "From her cache pit." The cache pit was a jug-shaped pit within or without the lodge, six or eight feet deep. It was floored with willow sticks and its walls were lined with dry grass. It was used to store the fall harvest.

Strings of braided ears were laid in series against the wall. Within these was poured the threshed grain, in which were buried strings of dried squash and sacks of beans and sunflower seed. Buffalo-Bird Woman says there were five cache pits in use in her father's family.

Many families had a cache pit within the lodge to serve as a cellar. Besides corn for immediate use, it held sacks of dried berries, prairie turnips, packages of dried meat and even bladders of marrow fat.

The pits without the lodge with their stores of grain were carefully sealed with slabs and grass, over which were trampled earth and ashes. This was done to conceal the pits from any Sioux who might come prowling around when the tribe was away in winter camp. If a family lacked food in winter, they returned to their summer village and opened one of these cache pit granaries for its stores of corn.

Page 49, l. 31: "Red Blossom pounded the parched corn ... in a corn mortar." The corn mortar, or hominy pounder, is a section of a cottonwood or ash trunk, hollowed out by fire. The pestal is of ash. The mortar was sunk in the floor of the earth lodge and covered, when not in use, by a flat stone.

Corn mortars are still used by the Hidatsas. Our grandmothers in pioneer days also used them.

Page 51, l. 4: "Chief." A Hidatsa chief, as explained, was not necessarily a tribal officer. His position was like that of an influential citizen of a country village, who is often a member of the local school or hospital board, is chosen to preside at patriotic meetings, and is expected to extend hospitality and charity to those in need.

Hospitality, indeed, is the Indian's crowning virtue. In tribal days, when one had food, all had food; when one starved, all starved. A reservation Indian does not like to take pay for a meal, especially from one of his own race; and he can not comprehend how any white man having food can let another go hungry.

His hospitality is often a hindrance to the Indian's progress. Indolent Indians eat up the food stores of industrious relatives.

Page 56, l. 14: "Dried meat pounded fine and mixed with marrow fat." This was regarded as a delicate dish. Old people especially were fond of it. The plains Indians usually had sound teeth, but their coarse diet wore the teeth down so that old men found it hard to eat dried meat unless it was thus pounded to shreds. Marrow fat was used much as we use butter.

Page 57, l. 1: "A doll, woven of rushes." Very good mats were also woven of rushes.

Page 58, l. 4: "Tossing in a blanket." The blanket tossing game has been found among widely separated peoples. In Don Quixote, we are told how Sancho Panza unwilling participated in the game.

Page 66, l. 6: "Every Hidatsa belonged to a clan." The clan was, nevertheless, relatively weak among the Hidatsas, its functions apparently having been usurped at least in part by the age societies. (The Black Mouths were an age society. See chapter V).

In many tribes a man was forbidden to marry within his clan.

Page 68, l. 25: "He was a great medicine man." The story of Snake Head-Ornament is a good example of the tales told of the old time medicine men. Snake Head-Ornament's friendship for the bull snake would seem uncanny even to a white man.

Page 73, l. 1: "In old times we Indian people had no horses."

At the time of America's discovery the Indians had domesticated the llama in the Peruvian highlands; the guinea pig, raised for food by many South American tribes; turkeys, and even bees, in Mexico; dogs, developed from wolves or coyotes, were universally domesticated among the North American tribes.

Indian dogs were used as watch dogs and as beasts of burden. Dog flesh was eaten by many tribes. An edible, hairless variety of dog, bred by the Mexican Indians has become extinct.

Page 77, l. 23: "My grandmother brought in some fresh sage." The sage was a sacred plant.

Page 81, l. 10: "Our dogs dragged well-laden travois." Older Indians say that a well-trained dog could drag a load of eighty pounds on a travois.

Page 85, l. 6: "The big tendon ... we Indians call the *eetsuta*."[34] When dried this tendon becomes hard, like horn; and arrow points and even arrow shafts were carved from it.

[34] ēēt sụ´ tä

Page 87, l. 32: "Coyote Eyes, a Ree Indian." The Rees, or Arikaras, are an offshoot of the Pawnee tribe, whose language they speak. They removed to Fort Berthold reservation and settled there with the Hidatsas and Mandans in 1862.

Page 92, l. 7: "To embroider with quills of gull." The tribe used to make annual journeys to the lakes near Minot, North Dakota, where, older Indians say, the gulls nested. The feathers were gathered along the beach. The quill was split, the flat nether half being the part used. Quills were dyed with native vegetable colors.

Page 99, l. 10: "Bear Man was an eagle hunter." The tail feathers of the golden eagle were much worn by all the plains tribes. These feathers, in eagles under two years of age, are of a pure white, with dark brown or black tips, and were much prized. Eagle hunting was a highly honored occupation.

Page 112, l. 17: "The huskers came into the field yelling and singing." Buffalo-Bird Woman laughingly adds, that the yelling was by young men who wanted their sweethearts to hear their voices.

Page 114, l. 2: "The hollow buffalo hoofs rattled." The earth lodge door was a heavy buffalo skin, stretched when green on a frame of light poles. It was swung from the beam above by heavy thongs. The puncheon fire screen stood between it and the fireplace, about which the family sat or worked. As the moccasined tread of a visitor made little noise, a bunch or two of buffalo hoofs was hung to a bar running across the middle of the door.

The hoof was prepared by boiling and removing the pith. Its edges were then trimmed and a hole was cut in the toe. Through this hole a thong was run with a knotted end, to keep the hoof from slipping off. As the door dropped after an entering visitor, the hollow hoofs fell together with a clittering noise, warning the family.

Page 118, l. 28: "Hanging Stone." A literal translation of the Hidatsa word. It refers to a form of war club, a short stick, from an end of which swung a stone sewed in a piece of skin.

Page 125, l. 3: "With ankles to the right, as Indian women sit." A warrior sat Turkish fashion, or, often, squat-on-heels. An Indian woman sat with feet to the right unless she was left-handed, when feet were to the left.

Page 125, l. 6: "Mixed with marrow fat." Marrow fat was obtained by boiling the crushed bones of a buffalo in a little water. The yellow marrow as it rose was skimmed off and stored in bladders or short casings made of entrails, like sausage casings.

Page 126, l. 10: "I have come to call you." Buffalo-Bird Woman means that her father invited his son-in-law to come and live in his earth lodge. If he had not sent this invitation, the young couple would have set up housekeeping elsewhere.

Page 128, l. 37: "Only a strong, well-fed pony could go all day on wet ground." Nature designed the solid hoof of the horse for a prairie or semidesert country. A pony finds it hard to withdraw his hoof in wet spongy soil, and soon tires. A deer or buffalo, with divided hoof, runs upon wet ground with comparative ease. Every farmer's boy knows that an ox will walk through a swamp in which a horse will mire.

Page 142, l. 26: "With two fingers crooked like horns, the sign for buffaloes." So many languages were spoken by our Indian tribes, that they found it necessary to invent a sign language so that Indians, ignorant of each other's speech, could converse. A well-trained deaf mute and an old plains Indian can readily talk together by signs.

Page 143, l. 4: "Creeping up the coulees." A coulee in the Dakotas is a grassy ravine, usually dry except in spring and autumn, and after a heavy rain.

Page 157, l. 19: "They starved, because they are hunters and raise no corn." The Hidatsas and Mandans as agriculturists felt themselves superior to the hunting tribes. Small-Ankle refers here to the western, or Teton, Sioux. The eastern Sioux were corn raisers.

Page 158, l. 10: "My mothers and I were more than a week threshing." In the summer of 1912, the author had Buffalo-Bird Woman pace off on the prairie the size of her mothers' field, as she recollected it. It measured one hundred and ninety yards in length by ninety yards in width. Such were some of the fields which in olden days were cultivated with wooden sticks and bone hoes.

SUPPLEMENT

HOW TO MAKE AN INDIAN CAMP

Young Americans who wish to grow up strong and healthy should live much out of doors; and there is no pleasanter way to do this than in an Indian camp. Such a camp you can make yourself, in your back yard or an empty lot or in a neighboring wood.

The Lodge

Buffalo-Bird Woman has told us of the earth lodges of her people. They were for permanent abode. Hunters, however, camping but a day or two in a place, usually put up a pole hunting lodge.

Four forked poles were stacked, as in Figure 1.

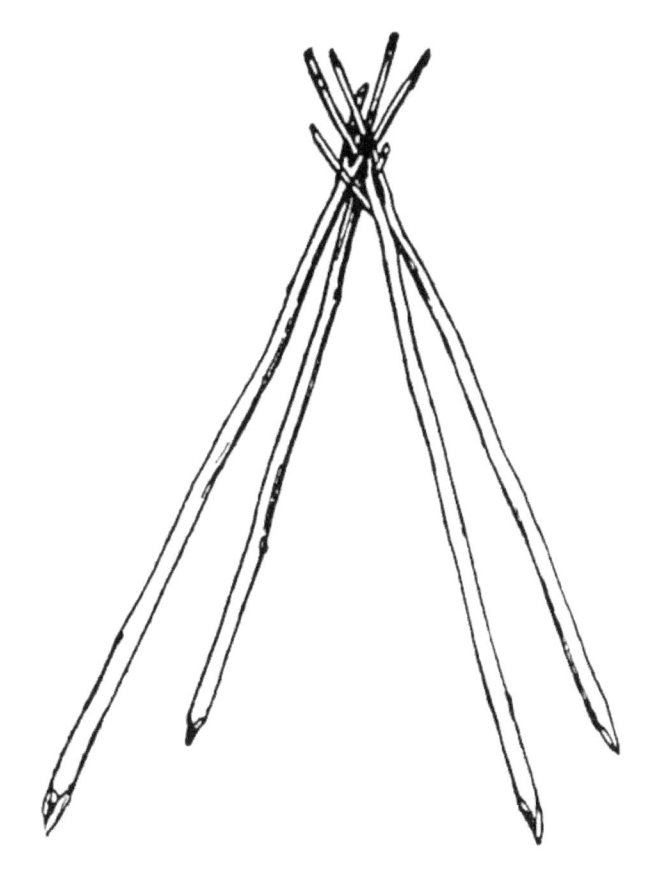

Figure 1

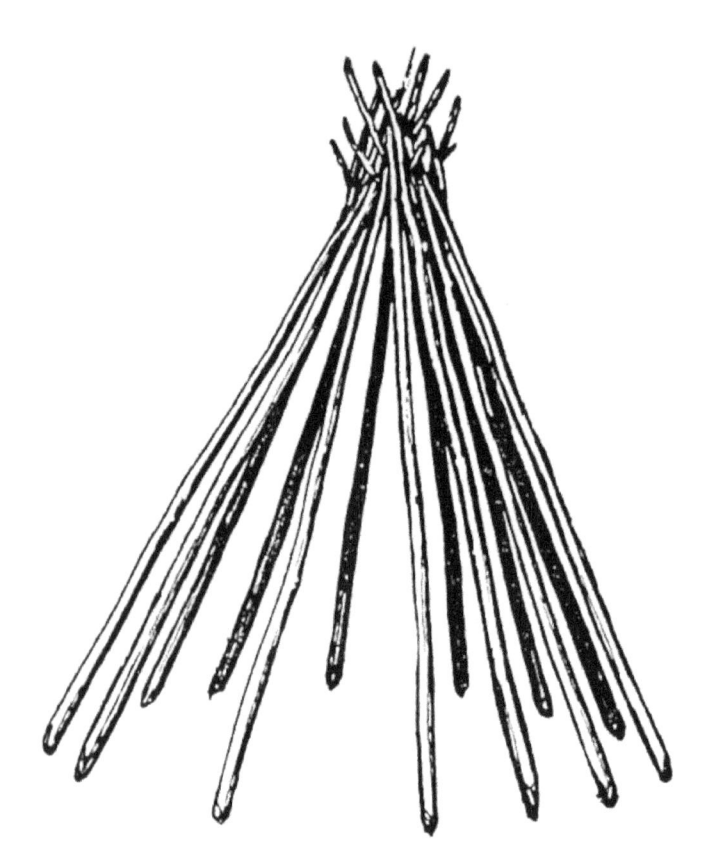

Figure 2

Around these in a circle, other poles were laid, as in Figure 2, for a frame.

For cover buffalo skins, bound together at the edges, were drawn around the frame in two series, the lower series being laid first. The peak of the pole frame was left uncovered, to let out the smoke.

Instead of buffalo skins, gunny sacks may be used, fastened at the edges with safety pins or with wooden skewers; or strips of canvas or carpet may be used. Three or four heavier poles may be laid against the gunny-sack cover to stay it in place.

The door may be made of a gunny sack, hung on a short pole.

Indians often raised a piece of skin on a forked pole for a shield, to keep the wind from driving the smoke down the smoke hole.

Figure 3 shows the finished lodge with gunny-sack cover, door, and wind shield. The last is made of a piece of oil cloth.

Figure 3

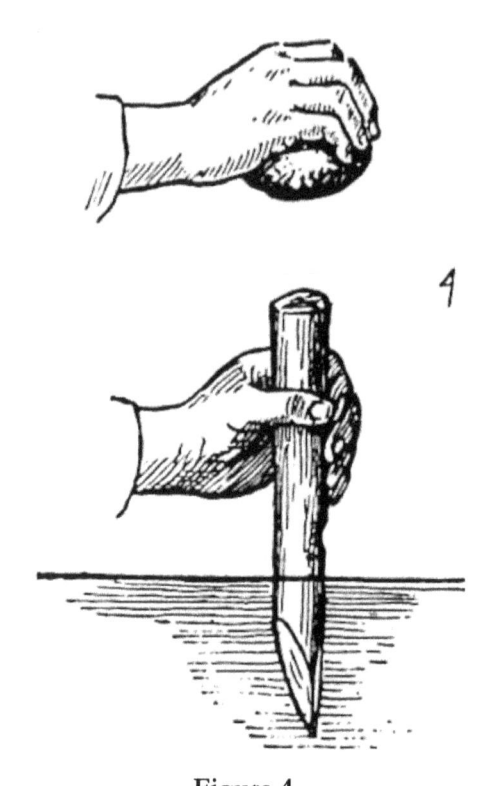

Figure 4

Booth

Buffalo-Bird Woman tells of the booth which Turtle made in her cornfield. A booth is easily made of willows or long branches.

A short digging stick will be needed. This was of ash, a foot or two in length, sharpened at one end by burning in a fire. The point was often rubbed with fat and charred over the coals to harden it. (Such a digging stick was not the kind used for cultivating corn.)

Figure 5

Figure 6

If you have no ash stick, a section of a broom handle will do.

With a stone, drive the digging stick four inches in the ground, as in Figure 4. Withdraw digging stick and repeat until you have six holes set in a circle. The diameter of the circle should be about five feet.

Into the six holes set willows, or branches, five or six feet high, as in Figure 5.

Weave or bind tops together so as to make a leafy roof, or shade, as in Figure 6. For binding, use strips of elm bark; or slender willows, twisted, so as to break the fibers.

Fireplace

Indians, when journeying, made the campfire outside the lodge in summer; inside the lodge, in winter. Usually a slight pit was dug for the fireplace, thus lessening danger of sparks, setting fire to prairie or forest. The fire was smothered with earth when camp was forsaken.

Figure 7

Figure 8

Broiling Meat

Indians broiled fresh meat on a stick thrust in the ground and leaning over the coals. Often a forked stick was cut, the meat was laid on the prongs, and it was held over the coals until broiled. In Figures 7 and 8 both methods are shown.

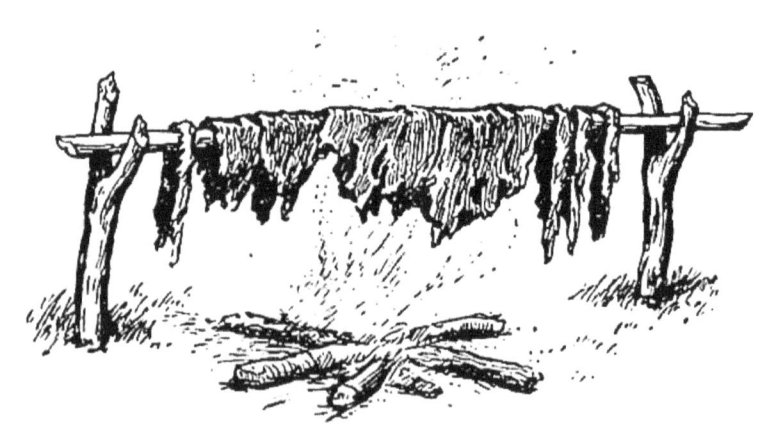

Figure 9

Drying Meat

Buffalo-Bird Woman often speaks of dried buffalo meat. If you want to know what it was like, cut a steak into thin pieces, and dry on a stage of green sticks, three feet high. This may be done in the sun; or, a small fire may be made beneath, to smoke as well as dry the meat. In Figures 9 and 10 two forms of drying stage are shown.

Figure 10

Cooking Dried Meat

A pail or small bucket will do for kettle. It should be swung from a tripod by stick-and-thong, as in Figure 11. Put in dried meat with enough water to cover, and bring to a boil. The broth may be used as the Indians used it, for a drink.

Parching Corn

Ripe sweet corn, thoroughly dried, is best for parching; but field corn will do nearly as well. Drop a handful of the shelled corn in a skillet with a little butter. Cover skillet and set on the fire. Shake skillet from side to side to keep corn from scorching.

In the earth lodge, Hidatsa women parched the grain in an earthen pot, stirring it with a stick. Indian boys, when out herding horses, often carried two or three ears of corn for lunch. An ear was parched by thrusting a stick into the cob, and holding it over the coals, as in Figure 12.

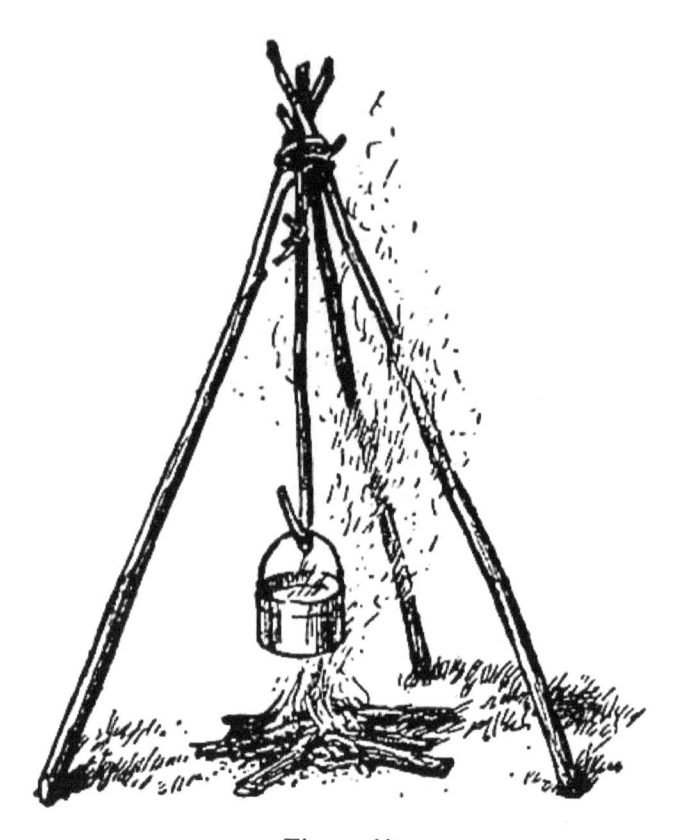

Figure 11

Figure 12

A steak broiled Indian fashion over the coals, or a kettle of boiled dried meat, with a cupful of parched corn, will make just such a meal as Indians often ate.

HINTS TO YOUNG CAMPERS

Do not throw away bits of unused food, but burn or bury them. Unless thus destroyed, the decaying food will attract insects, which often bring disease. Bury all tin cans.

Potatoes may be kept fresh as in your cellar by burying them in loose earth or sand.

Hang out your blankets and bed clothing to be aired an hour or two each day, preferably in the morning.

Indians had no soap. Indian women scoured out their earthen cooking pots with rushes. You may clean your camp kettle and pans in the same way; or, if no rushes can be found, scour with coarse grass dipped in wet sand or sandy mud, and drench with clean water.

Axes, clothing, shoes, and the like may be stored out of the way by making them into a long bundle, with a cloth or thick paper, and lashing them to one of the upright tent poles within the tent.

Indian children were fond of chewing green cornstalks, for the sweet juice they contained. If your camp is near a cornfield about the time the corn is in milk, you will find the chewed stalks almost as sweet as some varieties of sugar cane.

INDIAN COOKING

Young people often wonder what Indian cooking is like, and groups of them—as a class in Sunday school or day school—may like to eat a meal of Indian foods. Following are a few common Hidatsa dishes. Usually, but one kind of food was eaten at a single meal.

Madapozhee Eekteea[35], *or Boiled Whole Corn*

Pour three pints of water into a kettle and set on the fire. Drop in a pint of shelled field corn, a handful of kidney beans and a lump of suet the size of an egg. Boil until the corn kernels burst open.

[35] Mä dä pō´ zhēē Ēēk tēē´ ä

Manakapa[36], *or Mush*

Put a pint of shelled field corn into a canvas cloth, and with ax or stone pound to a coarse meal; or the corn may be ground in a coffee mill. To this meal add a handful of kidney beans, and boil in two pints of water. The Hidatsa mortar for pounding corn into meal is shown in cut on page 156.

[36] Mä´ nä kä pä

Dried, or Jerked, Meat

Cut some beefsteak, round or sirloin, into thin strips. Dry the strips on a stage of small poles (see cut on page 141) in the open air or over a slow fire, or in the kitchen oven, until brittle and hard. Meat thus dried could be kept for months. Warriors and hunters often ate jerked meat raw or toasted over a fire. In the lodge, it was more often boiled a few minutes to soften it; and the broth was drunk as we drink coffee. (See also "Drying Meat", page 185.)

Pemmican

Take strips of beef, dried as described above, and pound them to shreds between two hard stones. Put the shredded mass in a bowl, and pour over it a little marrow fat from a boiled soup bone, or some melted butter.

Corn Balls

The Hidatsas raised sweet corn for parching. Hunters often carried a pouch of the parched grain for a lunch. Parched ripe sweet corn was often pounded to a fine meal, kneaded with lumps of hot roasted suet, and rolled between the palms into little lumps, or balls, the size of one's thumb.

Hidatsa custom did not permit a woman to speak to her son-in-law; but she often showed her love for him by making him a bowl of corn balls.

EDITOR'S NOTE

Surrounded by the powerful and hostile Sioux, the two little Hidatsa tribes were compelled to keep relatively close to their stockaded villages and cornfields, which, however, they most sturdily defended. Their weakness proved a blessing. The yearly crops of their cornfields were a sure protection against famine, and in their crowded little villages was developed a culture that was remarkable. The circular earth lodges of the Mandans and Hidatsas represent the highest expression of the house-building art east of the Rocky Mountains.

Three members of Small Ankle's family are now living: Small Ankle's son, Wolf Chief, his daughter, Waheenee, or Buffalo-Bird Woman, and her son, Good Bird, or Goodbird. Goodbird was the first Indian of his tribe to receive a common school education. Like many Indians he has a natural taste for drawing. Several hundred sketches by him, crude but spirited and in true perspective, await publication by the Museum.

Goodbird's mother, Waheenee, is a marvelous source of information of old-time life and belief. Conservative, and sighing for the good old times, she is aware that the younger generation of Indians must adopt civilized ways. Ignorant of English, she has a quick intelligence and a memory that is marvelous. The stories in this book, out of her own life, were told by her with other accounts of scientific interest for the Museum. In the sweltering heat of an August day she has continued dictation for nine hours, lying down but never flagging, when too weary to sit longer in a chair. She is approximately 83 years old.

The stories in this book are true stories, typical of Indian life. Many of them are exactly as they fell from Waheenee's lips. Others have been completed from information given by Goodbird and Wolf Chief, and in a few instances by other Indians. The aim has been not to give a biography of Waheenee, but a series of stories illustrating the philosophy, the Indian-thinking of her life.

In story and picture, therefore, this book is true to fact and becomes not only a reader of unusual interest but a contribution to the literature of history and of anthropology. The author and the artist have expressed and portrayed customs, places, and things that are purely Indian and perfect in every detail.